BEFORE EMPIRE

RAISING
BRYSHERE "YAZZ THE GREATEST" GRAY

ANDRIA MAYBERRY
WITH MYA KAY

THE TMG FIRM

New York

The TMG Firm, LLC
112 W. 34th Street
17th and 18th Floors
New York, NY 10120
www.thetmgfirm.com

Before Empire: Raising Bryshere "Yazz The Greatest" Gray
Copyright © 2016 Andria Mayberry
© 2016 Mya K. Douglas
Published and edited by The TMG Firm, LLC

For more information about special discounts for bulk purchase, please contact The TMG Firm at 1-888-984-3864 ext 12 or
publishing@thetmgfirm.com

ISBN: 978-0-99835-6549
Library of Congress Control Number: 2016963015
All rights reserved

First The TMG Firm Trade Paperback Edition April 2017
Printed in the United States of America

This is a work of creative nonfiction. The events are portrayed to the best of Andria Mayberry's memory. The conversations in this book all come from the author's recollections, though they are not written to represent word-for-word transcripts. Rather, the author has retold them in a way that evokes the feeling and meaning what was said and in all instances, the essence of the dialogue is accurate. While all the stories in this book are true, some names and identifying details have been changed to protect the privacy of the people involved.

Cover Photo Copyright © 2016 Michael Moore
Cover created and designed by Brittani Williams for
TSPub Creative, LLC.

For Brianna and Yazz

Thank you to my family, friends and industry family for all of your support.

—Andria Mayberry

Thank You, Lord!

FOREWORD

My mother is the first example of sacrifice I've ever seen. She's always represented strength and grace, and I appreciate everything she's ever done for my sister Brianna and me. As far back as I can remember, I've seen my mother fight for us to have clothes, food and a warm place to lay our heads. Sometimes, that meant she had to work two jobs, but she did what she had to do. She stopped pursuing her dreams temporarily to make sure we could follow ours. When I decided I wanted to become an entertainer, she took it a step further and became my manager, so I had someone in my corner who always had my best interest at heart. She wore so many hats. From being my stage manager, tour manager, handling all of my promotions, choreography, and the list goes on. I wouldn't be who I am today without her love and sacrifices. The world wouldn't know Hakeem. Even though there were things I didn't always understand, I know, in the end, she did what was best for me. My mother taught me how to pray, how to put my faith in God and how to keep my family first. No matter what I go through in life, career changes and all, I know my mother will always be there to love, protect and pray for me. My prayer for her is that everyone appreciates what she sowed into my life before *Empire*. This is her story, and I'm sure you'll appreciate her journey after reading it.

I love you Mom!

—Yazz the Greatest

PART ONE

BRYSHERE

CHAPTER ONE

Sometimes, I wonder how it all happened. *Was I rushing my life or was God planning to give me a child He knew would be a big star one day? Could it be the plan was unfolding just the way He designed it?* I had a bunch of thoughts running through my mind when I had Bryshere, but regret was never one of them.

As a teenager in high school, I visited my cousin Lisa at the end of each week. One weekend, she introduced me to the brother of a guy she was dating. From then on, I visited every weekend to spend time with him. This is where my journey into entertainment all began. The guy I was dating started rapping while he was in high school. He released a single that became very popular, which secured him a record deal with a major label. At a young age, he performed at numerous shows that my cousin and I attended. I began to notice that I wasn't the only female he showed attention. He tried to explain that they were only fans, but I knew that wasn't the case. These girls were relentless and tried to get backstage by any means necessary. Then, he made up excuses as to why he couldn't leave with us after the shows so that he could spend time with other women. As a result, I decided to end the relationship because I didn't want to date someone that had multiple women. I knew my worth. Shortly thereafter, I met the father of my daughter Brianna.

He and I were young when we dated, so he was cheating, and our relationship ended. After a while, I reconnected with my ex. I tried to restore what we had and hoped that he would only have eyes for me, but after a few dates, I noticed he hadn't changed. He still wasn't ready to be monogamous and commit to being with only me. I then decided to remain as mutual friends.

This caused me to reevaluate the relationship between Brianna's father and me. I weighed the pros and cons, then finally decided to give him another chance to prove he had changed. During our reconnection period, I learned I was two months pregnant. When I told him, he seemed to be happier than I was. As time went on, I grew increasingly excited about having a baby. I was about nineteen when she was born, and working as a Certified Nursing Assitant. My position wasn't paying enough to take care of my family in the manner I wanted, so I began taking some pre-requisite nursing courses. I was a young girl in love, and I told myself the fairy tale wedding I'd dreamed of would come true one day. With the new found excitement for the baby came heartache from the relationship. My dreams of having a family with him were shattered when I discovered he was unfaithful again.

I realized that cheating was a pattern amongst the guys I was dating. I turned a blind eye to several instances of infidelity because I felt our 'puppy love' was real, and no one could convince me otherwise. My ex, was trying to rekindle our past, but I couldn't entertain him because I was with my daughter's father. I loved him, and in my heart I wanted our relationship to work. The harder I tried to hold on, the worse it became. So, when things turned tumultuous between us, and I was contemplating whether to stay or leave; my decision was made when I found out he had been arrested. At that point, I decided I would end our relationship and focus on how I was going to raise my daughter alone. That was the beginning of becoming a single parent.

Shortly after that, in 1992, I met Bryshere's father. I began thinking the dream of getting married and having a family wasn't so farfetched. I became pregnant with Bryshere when I was twenty. The way I learned that I was pregnant was during a visit to the doctor. I was battling a horrible case of chicken pox, and I couldn't take any medicine. The doctor asked me a few questions and then, had me take a pregnancy test. It was positive. All kinds of thoughts ran through my mind. I had anxiety about having another child. Here I was, about to have two children by the age of twenty-one and wasn't married to either of their fathers. My biggest hesitation came when my friends told me to reconsider having a child with his father. Rumors were circulating, and they heard about his abusive ways towards his ex-girlfriend. I told them I never witnessed any of that behavior from him. Unfortunately, I would soon learn that I spoke too soon.

There was a cloud of darkness that lingered in the air the day he beat me. At the time, I was seven months pregnant. What began as a great day, ended up being one of the worse days of my life. We went to breakfast and then decided to go shopping. We spent the entire day together, enjoying each other's company and conversing about the baby. We looked at baby items for Bryshere and even bought some things for my daughter. Later that evening, we stopped by his friend's house who was recently murdered. I wasn't feeling too well. I was ready to leave, but he wasn't ready to go. I could feel the exhaustion setting in, and I remember yawning a few times. When we got back into the car, the tension was noticeable immediately. We had an argument because he felt I had embarrassed him in front of his friend's family. Once he calmed down, he decided he wanted to make one more stop.

Once we finally made it to his place, I quickly went to lay down. He insisted on being intimate, but I wasn't feeling well, so I wasn't in the mood. I was lying on my back when all of a sudden, he jumped on top of me and proceeded to punch me! Every time he hit me, it felt like I was being run over by a truck. All I could do was shield my face and my stomach. When I tried to fight back, I immediately realized I wouldn't win. I couldn't beat a man, especially not in my condition. When the blows lessened, I was able to take a quick glance into his eyes. I didn't see Bryshere's father anymore; I was looking into the eyes of a demon. He turned into someone I didn't even recognize. He was an entirely different person and the rage in his eyes sent chills up my spine. The quick and increased anger reminded me of The Incredible Hulk. I fought as hard as I could, but couldn't get him off of me. The more I resisted, the tighter his grip became. Trying to kick him off of me even became a struggle. Then all of a sudden, there was loud banging at the door! I could see the door knob twist left and right as if someone was trying to enter the locked room. It was his mother and grandmother; I could hear their voices as they repeatedly asked me if I was okay. Thank God they were in the next room and heard my cries. My pleas for help didn't fall upon deaf ears. By now, I'm on the floor yelling at the top of my lungs, while the concerned screams accompanied by the banging on the door rang in my ears.

He finally stopped, after what felt like an eternity. He stood over me with guilt in his voice and pain in his eyes, as he apologized in a loud screaming tone repeating he would never hit me again. At that very moment, all I could think about was the condition of my face; *I want to see my face, I want to see my face,* is all I could think to myself. I could feel my face was severely swollen and I felt the blood dripping from my open wounds. When I finally mustered up the courage to look into the mirror, my face was disfigured, and I was missing a front tooth. It was so bad; I had to eat and drink through a straw for weeks. While going through this, I've already had in my mind that I was ending the relationship with him and never was I going to take him back. It only took one time to be abused for me to get the message. Due to the extent of my injuries, I clearly understood things would only get worse, so it was necessary to end the relationship. God knows I loved that man, but I loved my children more. I wanted to live and needed to live for them.

I was living with my mother and stepfather at the time, and I couldn't go home; I just couldn't face them and my daughter. Nor did I want to deal with all of the questions that would follow. When she didn't hear from me by eight the next morning, she knew exactly where to find me. She arrived at Bryshere's father's house and ever so politely, but passive-aggressively escorted me out. I didn't press charges against him. I couldn't because that's my son's father, but I did file a restraining order. I had to, for my protection, because I knew he wasn't going to change. For him to react that way, especially while I was carrying his son, let me know something deeper lied beneath his actions. I didn't have time to figure it out; I just knew I had to protect my children. I would never expose my kids to the treatment I received that night, so I dragged myself to the police station to get the restraining order. I remember the officer looking at me, wondering if I would enforce the order of protection or change my mind and not go through with it. When I felt Bryshere kick, it was a sign. It was now or never! I knew there was no way I would change my mind.

The stress from the beating induced a premature labor. I was twenty-one and delivered Bryshere on November 28, 1993, even though my due date was December thirteenth. Despite everything his father took me through, I allowed him to be in the room while I gave birth, to witness his son being born. I was having a baby boy and wanted to share that experience with him since he was his father. I wanted him to be in his life. I needed Bryshere to know him. This was an amends for us, so he could be there and be better for Bryshere, even though we were no longer together. I only had one rule, and that was I had to be present when he was with our son. The things I continued to hear along with new information about him made me very uncomfortable. Because of that, I knew I always needed to be there when they were together.

As soon as he was born, they immediately transferred him to the Children's Hospital of Philadelphia because he had complications breathing. He remained in the hospital for four days. Every day, I visited my son in the hospital faithfully. I was always escorted by someone because I was terrified of being alone in the room with Bryshere if his father showed up unannounced. He had rights too, so I couldn't deny him visitation. But I needed to be prepared; I couldn't take the chance of him catching me off guard.

While our son was still in the hospital, his father called me to discuss how we could co-parent. The conversation didn't go as expected, but I didn't think anything of it. As he continued to speak, he stopped mid-sentence and demanded me to meet him around the corner to further the discussion in person. When I met with him, I was shaking uncontrollably. I felt something was strange as soon as I walked around the corner. As he approached me, his conversation went from positive to negative. Looking into his eyes reminded me of the rage I had previously witnessed. He started to form his hands into fists, and he became enraged and out of control. He threw me onto the ground and began kicking me as hard as he could! He continuously kicked and stomped me with no remorse.

When he finally became too tired to continue, he spat on me with disgust. He threatened to kill me, and in a vengeful tone yelled, "You're not leaving me!" I was on the ground in so much pain as I lay in the fetal position, trying to protect myself. Somehow, I gained enough courage to cry for help with the little energy I thought I didn't have. Then, all of a sudden I belted out in screams. I started screaming, I mean gut wrenching screams. Although no one was outside while we were arguing and fighting, like a miracle, from out of nowhere, two guys who were like my brothers came rushing down the street. They started cursing and yelling while running toward us. Bryshere's father took off running. Being more concerned with me, they didn't chase him but instead stayed and asked if I was okay. I didn't want them to chase after him; I only wanted to be walked home to ensure I was safe.

Even after both brutal beatings, I knew there was no way I could keep his son away from him. I had to figure out how to co-parent with him, so I made the decision to set up supervised visits. Someone always had to be present for him to see his son. I didn't feel safe, and with his frequent unpredictable outbursts of violence, it was clear I couldn't trust him. Unfortunately, we were unable to come to a realistic plan to co-parent. So, just like that; his father was gone.

***

Bryshere didn't learn how to walk until he was about thirteen months old, so he crawled everywhere. Even when he learned how to walk, he reverted to crawling. He kept a pacifier in his mouth for quite a while. I even had to pry it from between his teeth to take it away from him.

To make matters worse, Bryshere was diagnosed with asthma. He started having issues immediately, and I didn't fully understand his breathing complications. I took him to the hospital, but they discharged him without any reassurance of his condition improving. They only gave me a nebulizer machine and sent me on my way. Trying to figure out how to properly use the nebulizer became increasingly frustrating. It was a foreign object to me and learning how to use it with the instructions gave me anxiety. Once I finally figured it out, I had to explain it to my family thoroughly. They needed to know the implementation process, to provide him with the best care while they watched him.

It was rough raising a boy alone. He required around the clock treatments, and I juggled it all while taking care of my two-year-old daughter. It was a challenge, but it had to be done. I was determined not to let this break me, so I put forth my strongest effort and became even stronger. As a single parent who was not receiving assistance from either of my children's fathers, I knew that I needed more. I re-enrolled in school to pursue a career in nursing. I was a non-traditional student whose path to a degree was also non-traditional. There were times during my enrollment that I had to step away from classes and focus on working. While school would get me to where I wanted to be, there was no doubt that my job kept me where I needed to be at the moment. It was never an easy decision to step away from my pursuit of a nursing degree, but it was best for my family and me. I always put my faith in God, so the future appeared more promising.

***

At the age of five, he started to have trouble at school. He was persistent and adamant about not having his treatments while in school. Often, I left work early to visit his school to make sure he had his treatments.

During this time, his teachers began to notice other changes. I began receiving phone calls regularly about his behavior. They informed me that he would abruptly walk out of the classroom or be disruptive while the teacher was conducting the class. He constantly wanted to play around and never wanted to sit still during the lesson. On one particular day, when I arrived at his school to pick him up, the teacher insisted we have a quick conversation about his behavior. By now, this was the norm and an everyday occurrence. But this time something wasn't right, she seemed a little more concerned than before. His teacher began the conversation hesitantly and then informed me that she and the school faculty insisted Bryshere be evaluated for ADHD, Attention-deficit/hyperactivity disorder, a chronic condition marked by persistent inattention, hyperactivity, and sometimes impulsivity. "ADHD?" I repeated. The condition begins in childhood, but there was no way my son had a disorder. I didn't accept what she said, so I didn't pay it much mind. I took my son home and continued our usual routine. Even though I brushed off that conversation, it still lingered in the back of my mind for quite some time.

One day, I received a disturbing phone call from his teacher. She was so upset; I had to calm her down so that I could clearly understand what she was trying to tell me. She just kept saying, "You have to come get him, you have to come get him!" She was practically begging and pleading with me to pick him up from school. At the end of the phone call, she said I needed to pick him up from school immediately, and I needed to attend an emergency meeting. I remember different thoughts running through my mind. *Why are they singling out my son? Other students in his class act like him. Why does he have to be evaluated?* I was at a loss for words when I arrived at the school. As I stood staring at this Caucasian teacher, looking like she was scared for her life, I began to think maybe she was discriminating against Bryshere. She was a Caucasian teacher, dealing with a bunch of African American kids in the heart an impoverished neighborhood. I thought to myself; *Maybe she just doesn't understand my son.* I convinced myself that had to be the real issue, as we walked silently to the principal's office. It was at that time; the principal said he couldn't return to school unless he were evaluated.

The news hit me like a ton of bricks. I went into defense mode, as any mother would. But my argument was quickly cut short, as the teacher explained why this was necessary. She went on to say, most of her frustration was getting him to focus when it was time to do his assignments. He would become extremely active and disruptive, sending the other students into an uproar leaving her in tears at her desk. Although I sympathized with her as she gave me examples of how Bryshere made it difficult for her to do her job; I didn't feel comfortable with the school being so quick to diagnose him. I saw it happen far too many times with African American inner city kids. Someone loses their patience with a child, decides something must be wrong with them, and medication is the solution. I wasn't going to let that happen to my son, so I made a decision that I was going to have him properly evaluated. I had to find out what was wrong with him and make sure he received the help he needed. I had already prepared myself on how to protect him from the streets and people who might try to hurt him. Nothing could've prepared me for what I would endure when dealing with his ADHD.

When I decided to have him evaluated, I was still in denial. I prolonged arranging the appointment because I felt his behavior was normal for a child his age. However, the school didn't leave me any other options, so I had to have him examined. My mother sided with the teacher and also suggested I have him assessed. Hearing that my son could have ADHD had me afraid and confused. The most important question I thought was, *What does all this mean for him?* I didn't know how it would affect him as a child or in the future. I embraced it as a negative situation and took it day by day. My perception of the teachers was that they were attempting to get rid of him because he was what some would call "a problem child." I took it personally and felt attacked. But when his disruptive behavior turned into excessive fighting I buckled down and made the appointment sooner than later. When Bryshere was first diagnosed, I had to take it seriously immediately. They placed him on medication and recommended I have him attend therapy once a week.

When he was six years old, I decided to enroll him in a football program. I learned about it through his daycare provider's daughter, whose son attended the same daycare center. I was apprehensive at first because I was worried about him having an asthma attack on the field. However, I knew football was the significant help he needed in his life mentally and physically.

I witnessed firsthand how football helped him exert all of his energy. By the time he arrived home from practice or a game, he would have just enough energy to do his homework and prepare for the next day. Before he started playing football, I spoke with his coaches to help them to understand his behavior and educate them about his ADHD. When he was disruptive, they would discipline him by sitting him on the bench. I asked the coaches if they could find another way to discipline him; a way that would allow him to play still. Because benching him was not going to teach him a lesson, he would only distract the players on his team from the sideline. Besides, there's way no way that he would be able to sit all of that time, it was just something he couldn't do. Making him run laps would be a more adequate punishment. He was the star running back every year he played, and the coaches recognized that he was gifted. So, I wanted him to showcase his talents and being benched prevented that. Eventually, I enrolled him in a basketball and track program as well. Track helped him build the stamina he needed for football. I still have all of his MVP plaques and trophies he won as a star athlete.

I noticed when Bryshere was doing something he enjoyed or did well; he performed better at everything else. It was clear that playing sports gave him focus. I also think it helped him release any suppressed energy from sitting in school all day. As he continued to excel in sports, I realized he needed his father there to support him. It took a few years for me to tell his father about the ADHD. I was still in communication with his father's mother. I always had a good relationship with her, and she checked on her grandson all the time.

***

At the time, I was living with my mother and stepfather. Whenever my son was with her, she created things for him to do because he was so busy and active. She was a huge part of his life because she was his caregiver. She felt at peace sitting him in front of the television and not allowing anyone to change the channel. She dealt with his ADHD as best she could. My stepfather didn't like hearing the noise Bryshere made, so much of her day consisted of her trying to keep him calm. I was grateful that she was there when I needed her.

While I was sincerely appreciative of her assistance, I was determined to find a place for my children. I wanted, and they deserved a more stable living situation. Truthfully, my income at the time posed a given set of challenges; however, it wasn't long before I was able to get an apartment in Haines Street projects, in Germantown, a section of Northwest Philadelphia.

Bryshere was seven, and we were on welfare. In my new place, I was only responsible for paying my monthly rent because utilities were included with subsidized housing. That was a financial blessing.

I was in fear when we lived there. Even when we moved to a different side of the projects, I was afraid to sleep at night. I didn't know if someone was going to try something because they knew I was a single mother. For my children, I was terrified and didn't want them to play outside. I didn't let them out of my sight, and they couldn't go outside without me. Everything from drug dealing to gun violence surrounded us. There was a young guy killed up the street, and right then I knew had to get myself together. With my son living in that environment as a young black male, I didn't want him to meet the same fate. I refused to have my daughter become a teenage mother as I had been. To put my plan in motion, I once again withdrew from school and went back to work to save money.

***

Years after his father and I ended our relationship; I learned some very interesting information. I was informed by Bryshere's grandmother that his father had schizophrenia. This is what they believed, although he'd never been diagnosed officially. She also let me know she was diagnosed with ADHD and was prescribed medication to keep it under control. After learning all this new information, I knew I had to inform his father about his son's condition even though we didn't have a cordial relationship.

Bryshere's father was traveling back and forth from Atlanta to Philadelphia often, so I hadn't let him know the issue with his son. One day I was at his mother's house visiting her, and I finally decided to break the news about the ADHD to his father. He denied it right away and said, "There's nothing wrong with that boy." I couldn't believe he didn't ask me any questions. He didn't even ask if I needed anything to help Bryshere; he just flat out denied it. Bryshere's father had issues to deal with himself, such as being verbally and mentally abusive. He was even verbally abusive toward his mother at times. When he acted that way in front of my son, it was too much for him to handle as a child.

I remember one weekend, my son's grandmother called and asked if he could come over to her house to play with the other children. She had two younger children there that were about his age. She also let me know his father would be there as well. I told her it would be all right, as long as she was there the entire time. A few hours later, Bryshere called me very upset and wanted me to pick him up. At that point, he didn't like cigarette or marijuana smoke around him, and his father was a smoker. This worried me because the smoke could trigger his asthma. He also told me his father was mean, so he didn't feel comfortable being there. He said he asked his father to stop smoking around him, but his father said, "I'm grown and can smoke if I want to."

As he continued to smoke, Bryshere told him that he couldn't breathe. I guess he didn't like the tone of his voice, so he told him to get away from him, or he would beat his ass. When I arrived, his father and I exchanged words. I asked him to step outside to speak privately because he had guests in the house. I was afraid to be alone with him, but thinking about my son diminished all of my fears. When I tried to explain Bryshere's condition, he rudely interrupted and said, "Ain't nothing wrong with him. He's just too damn grown!" He further proceeded with letting me know; I didn't have to bring him to visit anymore if I didn't want to. Once I realized he didn't care about our son, I told his mother I wasn't bringing Bryshere back until he moved out. I don't believe my son had the intention of disrespecting his father when he asked him to stop smoking around him. I think it came out wrong as most things did whenever he felt backed into a corner.

During the ride home, I spoke with him about it. He was still upset, and I told him no matter what happened he still had to respect his father. He kept asking me not to take him over there again. At that point, he didn't go back over there for a while, but I didn't prevent him from being around his aunts and uncles. His father had many brothers and sisters, and I never wanted to take them out of his life. My mindset was focused on protecting my son and making sure he was always fine, regardless of how others felt. Once Bryshere made that decision, I told him if he didn't go back to his grandmother's house, it would be difficult to see her. He told me that she could come to visit him. She didn't have a car, so I knew it was almost impossible. Bryshere kept saying, "If she wants to see me, she'll find a way." His grandmother had a good heart, and she loved him very much. She would teach him things and tell him all kinds of stories. I couldn't deny them from seeing each other, so I decided to take him to her house when his father wasn't there. I would stay with him so that she wouldn't feel punished for her son's actions.

At that time, his father may have been embarrassed with the negative connotation associated with his son being labeled, but Bryshere wasn't concerned about who knew about his condition. It wasn't discussed outside of the house, but it wasn't hidden like a secret either. After he had turned eight, he was concerned with people knowing about his disorder. He didn't want me visiting the school and saying certain things in front of the classroom. I never did that anyway. During one instance, a student overheard two teachers discussing my son. He was so bothered, that he didn't want to return to that classroom. His way of addressing it was to avoid it until something brought to his attention. It had become a defense mechanism of his.

Whenever a student started talking to him during class or he observed someone else being disruptive, that triggered his behavior. If he were bored or disinterested in the subject, he would find something else to occupy his time. I devised a plan to give him the initiative to be better. He loved money, so I gave him incentives like an opportunity to earn an allowance. I would allow him to travel the mall. As often as I could, I would let him know when he was doing the right things. I also encouraged the teachers to permit him to walk around the classroom if he finished his work early and to let him know he was doing a good job. That provided him with the positive reinforcement he needed.

I would incorporate some of the strategies that I gave the teachers at home, so he was in a consistent cultivating environment. Praise is crucial for a child with ADHD. Those acknowledgments meant the world to him. When I pointed out the things he did correctly, he continued to make me proud. He still had triggers at home from his sister picking on him or teasing him when he did get punished. They would especially get into a dispute when she lied and said he did something he didn't. If I believed her because of his past behaviors, that would make him very upset and withdrawn. That would result in him having a bad day at school the next day; making matters even worse.

I had an IEP established for him, which is an Individual Educational Plan that's developed to ensure that a child who has a disability identified under the law and is attending an elementary or secondary educational institution receives specialized instruction and related services. In other words, it's a contract between the school and the parent, which makes sure your child isn't left behind academically. The conditions stipulated that every teacher had to abide by the information included in the plan. For example, he was allotted additional time to take quizzes and exams. He was even able to walk around the classroom if necessary, especially if he sat too long. Even though I was still working two jobs, I was very committed to the IEP program. I made sure that anyone who had contact with my son, understood the importance of the program. More importantly, I let them know they would be held accountable for not upholding their duties. The good thing was that anyone who had interactions with him had to attend the meetings regarding the program with me.

The teachers would email me progress reports weekly. Since I had this new supplemental educational support, I needed to have my phone turned on while I was at work. I had a conversation with my boss, explaining the reason and assured her I would not let this be a distraction or interference. I agreed only to use my phone within the set guidelines. Then, out of nowhere, my daughter began having behavioral issues. She was doing well in school, but she and I began having verbal disputes. She also wanted to use the phone all hours of the night. I contributed it to her going through puberty. Even though we had a sit-down as a family and discussed the issues with Bryshere, she didn't fully understand ADHD. There were times both of them were experiencing behavioral issues during the same period. Because of her misunderstanding about his disorder, she felt he was just spoiled. I was exhausted mentally and physically. I needed support, so I asked my daughter to lend me her help as the big sister I needed her to be. She began to consent and checked on him to make sure he was fine. She always let me know when he was doing something that was inappropriate and unacceptable.

There were times that Brianna and Bryshere wouldn't speak to each other for extended periods. I would have to intervene and encourage them to discuss whatever their issue with the other was. We began the discussions with prayer, with the hopes of keeping the discussions civil, and to open our hearts to so that we get to the root of the problem. I would ask God for unity, love, peace and understanding in my household. I then would ask God to cover the house in his blood to help us have clear minds and open hearts. When the conversation began, we put all our feelings out in the open. I let them know that they could tell me anything, even if it was about me working too much.

When Brianna felt comfortable enough to speak, she asked why her father and I weren't together. Before I could answer, Bryshere repeated the same question about his father. In a previous discussion with his grandmother, she told him that his father was abusive and that was the reason his parents weren't together. He was upset after she told him that, but I guess he needed more answers. I didn't want to go into details about their fathers, so I told them their fathers had issues. I let both of them know that a man should never put his hands on a woman under any circumstances. It was imperative that my son knew not to abuse women and my daughter understood not to accept any abuse. I hoped the explanation I gave them about their fathers provided some closure, but it was clear they would need time to understand fully. All I could do was be honest and let them know that every decision I made was for all of us. I wanted my children to have an open and honest relationship with me. I never wanted them to seek other people to discuss any issues they experienced. I accepted that I needed to hear everything they had to say; even if it hurt my feelings.

At some point, Bryshere's father would call periodically to find out how he was doing. I took the initiative to invite him to his football games. I gave him all the information, such as the schedule and location of the games. I left it for him to decide if he was going to attend. Bryshere knew if no one else showed up; he always could count on my daughter and me to be in attendance. Sometimes, my mother would attend as a proud grandparent and record the games. I wanted to be both supportive and active at his games, so I volunteered at the concession stand. I worked long enough to lend my assistance, and then someone replaced me so that I could watch him play in the game.

As time went on, the absence of his father left a void in his heart. During his games, I noticed him looking around for his father. Most of the other kids had their fathers or male figures cheering them on, but he didn't. He was very excited at the beginning of the game; then his demeanor changed once he noticed he wasn't there. It was heart-wrenching witnessing him go through that pain. Despite their fathers being absent, I decided to keep them busy. That way, they could remain focused on things that made a positive impact in their lives. So, as they became older and were able to work, they worked as volunteers at my hospital during the summer for four hours a day. Then after they were done, they would participate in a youth program that was run by the city of Philadelphia for an additional four hours a day. For their efforts, they were paid.

I enrolled in school and became even busier as I juggled motherly duties, a course workload, and a full-time job. I left work early often, to make certain he arrived to football practice on time. I utilized the two hours I waited for him, by tirelessly working on assignments; many that were due the next day. Most nights, he didn't finish practice until eight. By the time he was finished, we didn't have much time to spare. When we arrived home, he had just enough time to do his homework, eat dinner and prepare for bed. Our day began at five every morning, so long nights often left us all exhausted.

No matter how busy, I would take the time to ask them how they were doing and coping with everything. I wanted to know how their day was and so forth. Being so busy didn't leave me with much time to date anyone. Whenever I did date, I did so outside of the house. When I went out, I only left them with my mother or a trusted babysitter. When I was fortunate enough to find a babysitter that wasn't family, I kept his disorder a secret. It wasn't the most honest of things to do, but at the time I was desperate. The secret didn't last long before the guilt sat in and I came to the conclusion that it was best to inform the babysitter of his condition as to avoid any possibility of any issue if his behavior spun out of control.

I didn't think to ask his father to care for him while I was out. There were so many questions that ran through my mind at the thought of even considering leaving our son in his care. Would he be in a rage and beat him like he beat me? His father was uneducated on his condition, and because he had his issues, I knew he couldn't be trusted. So, my mother was always there, watching them so I could work. I had to work sixteen-hour shifts, sometimes four times a week just to make ends meet.

I don't think there's one particular way for a single-parent to work multiple hours and be there for their children. I was doing it all because I wanted a better my life for my kids and me. I never made excuses as to why I couldn't finish school. I knew it might take a bit longer than others, but I was determined to finish. There were days I felt I was studying for school and studying for Bryshere. Learning more about his disorder was like constantly being in class. I had to learn quickly and teach those that interacted with him. I knew I had to keep going and pursue the things that would benefit all of us.

That's when I quickly learned there was more to combating ADHD than just medicine. The process was explained, but still, nothing prepares you for the battle until you're in it. I had to spend countless hours on the phone with patient advocates and discuss behavioral and educational plans with each of his teachers. Reluctantly, we went to therapy, and the tools they provided helped communicating with him much easier. They taught us hands on skills on how to interact and relay things to him in a certain way. This helped him comprehend what we were ultimately asking of him. Another positive about the therapy was it allowed us to have individual sessions as well as family group sessions. My daughter was included because I figured it was the best way to explain what was happening with her brother. She was constantly teasing him because he would often get into trouble. She didn't know his behavioral problems were linked to a disorder. Once she understood the underlying issue, it made it easier for us to deal with his condition. I knew I couldn't control children teasing him at school or in our neighborhood, but I could control what happened in my home.

Now that my household was in order, it provided me with time to focus on other challenges in my life, such as working two jobs as a single mother. In addition to, managing everything surrounding Bryshere and dealing with his asthma. Maintaining control of his ADHD was like having a third job. It required so much dedication I told myself over and over again things would get better. I even convinced myself having to work two jobs was something I had to do to provide for my children. It wasn't my kids' fault I had to work two jobs, and I didn't take it out on them. With all the stress sometimes it made it hard not to, at least not advertently. I found myself growing increasingly upset with him about little things. One time, he was coloring on a sheet of paper while propped against my brand new chair. I had just worked sixteen consecutive hours to pay for the chair. When I turned around and saw the color marks on it; I freaked out! I understood he was just a child and this particular behavior wasn't even associated with his disorder. I knew this was an honest mistake, but I was still furious. As I fussed, he and I began to scrub the color marks off the chair with a wet towel. I was so upset, I totally missed that he was going into, what therapy called "defense mode" because I reprimanded him in an aggressive tone.

I was conditioned to parenting the way I was raised. I had to adjust my methods to support the correct way to deal with his disorder. I knew I had to discipline my children, so they learned there were ramifications when they did something wrong. I just needed to learn the effective way to deal with each of them accordingly. My previous ways were making it worse, so I had to take a step back, regroup, and proceed with a new plan.

Sometimes, I was so focused on 'paying the bills' I didn't realize I was failing as a parent. I can recall times Bryshere was crying out for more of my attention, but I had to work. Even my daughter had moments where she felt I was neglecting them by working too much. I was accustomed to seeing single mothers struggle and work long hours at multiple jobs. When you have children, no one hands you a manual that teaches you how to be a parent; you learn through trial and error. My top priority was keeping them safe, providing the best I could and making sure they had everything they needed. Bryshere's condition brought its set of challenges. I took the time to learn everything I could about the disorder. His condition made me realize no matter how much I worked; I was the only one who cared enough to take the time to understand what he was experiencing. From therapy to individual educational plans, the journey with his ADHD was one that I will never forget.

CHAPTER TWO

Bryshere had his first therapy session when he was six. At this time, I knew I was doing the right thing by helping my son. I remember him clenching my hand tightly as we walked into the therapist's office. I could feel his energy - he was petrified. It was like he knew the reason we were there had something to do with him. I knew he didn't fully understand and I tried my best to keep him at ease while we attended that initial session and all those that were to follow. I felt alone while going through all of this. The situation began to worsen because I took too much time off work. To make ends meet, I had to work overtime. As we continued to attend his sessions, he began to make the therapy process difficult. He didn't like the therapists; he interpreted it as going to the doctor, which he despised. During our first visit, he didn't say anything to anyone when we came into the office. It took a few months for him to feel comfortable enough to open up and speak to the therapist. That's when he began to address the concerns he had with his father not being in his life. He was only scheduled to attend once a month, but sometimes I would take him twice a month if I felt he needed it. This was so he could convey his frustrations to the therapist to relieve some of that pent-up anger he held inside.

A part of me was afraid to attend therapy. I felt the therapist would judge and blame me for Bryshere's condition. I wasn't quite ready for the judgment I was certain she would disguise as a concern. I was even worried that if I told her I disciplined him before differentiating between his disorder and an act of bad behavior, she would consider reporting me to Child Services for abuse. This could mean possible jail time, and Bryshere hauled off to a foster home. Despite my fears, I knew the only way she could help me was if she knew the truth. I needed to be completely transparent, and the truth had to be revealed in each session; no matter the shame or embarrassment. The sessions helped me cope with the trials and tribulations of the ordeal. One of the things I learned, was I had to leave him alone for an hour whenever he acted out. When I began the sessions, I wasn't receptive to them, but soon realized I needed to try everything I could to help him. My goal was to do that successfully, but not frustrate myself at the same time. As we continued, the sessions became progressive. My mind and heart were open, so I was able to receive the information in the sessions differently. There were many times he wanted to cancel his sessions. I would have to threaten to take away football or any other extracurricular activities if he refused to attend. He felt he didn't need therapy as much because he believed he was getting better. I reminded him that going would help control his disorder and give him further success in his future.

Through it all, I always put God first in my life. I was down on my knees praying one night, calling out to God to help me understand what more I could do. I needed the wisdom I couldn't find in any of the books I had from the library or in any of the literature I received from the doctors. Prayer helped me accept that my son had a disorder. Even though time had passed, I still hadn't fully accepted it and struggled with getting him to embrace it as well. I found comfort in knowing that God doesn't make any mistakes and that something beautiful would come out of this. His father abused me, but he was my 'beautiful something' that came out of that horrible situation. Because of that, I knew God wouldn't let me down. I was always taught that "God doesn't put more on you than you can bear," and I lived by that creed.

As I gradually came to grips with everything, I was still battling with him to take his medication and adhere to his required schedule. At times, I would use a syringe to administer his medications because a missed day would disrupt our progress and send us back to step one. For some reason, this stressed me out more than when I learned about his ADHD. It was a constant roller coaster of ups and downs. I worried even more about how the teachers were treating him. *How was he behaving? Were they going to make up an excuse to expel him from school?* I was managing everything by myself, with minimal help from my family. I didn't think the stress could build anymore until I learned his asthma and ADHD could collide. In other words, if Bryshere became angry enough, it would trigger his asthma. If his nebulizer wasn't providing him the relief he needed, then I would have to rush him to the emergency room. This sent my stress levels through the roof and frightened me out of my mind.

On top of his conditions, he also had regular ear infections and multiple throat complications. When he slept at night, I always heard him struggling to breathe, so I slept with one eye opened and watched him like a hawk. There were many sleepless nights, but I would have done anything for his well-being. Eventually, the doctors identified his tonsils as the cause of his sore throats and breathing issues. I scheduled an appointment to have them removed, and that stopped the snoring, which caused his sore throats and breathing problems. If it wasn't one thing, it was another.

While the sore throats and ear infections subsided, there was one thing that would remain; the ADHD. I couldn't control it like I could his asthma and other minor ailments. With everything that was occurring, I also had a little brother and sister who were practically raised with Bryshere and Brianna. I had four kids looking up to me instead of two, so I felt like I had to be an example for all of them. Maybe, I was putting more on my shoulders than I needed. I guess that's why a part of me yearned to have a normal life to help escape the daily chaos.

***

Although I was a full-time parent, I was still trying to have a social life with my girlfriends and family. My cousin and I spent time in North Philadelphia, where we were raised, and I began dating someone I knew since childhood. Both of our families already knew each other because we were raised together in the same neighborhood, so our relationship gelled well. As the relationship progressed, we became engaged to be married. Mr. Billips became an excellent father figure to my children and was very active in Bryshere's life.

You would've thought he and I had created him together. There were many times my son wanted to spend more time with him than he wanted to spend with me. He was a huge help with addressing the multitude of things I dealt with on a daily basis. For instance, after he left work, he would pick up the kids from school, bring them home, prepare dinner, and assist them with their homework. By the time I arrived home after a long work day, everything was done, which was a tremendous burden lifted off my shoulders.

He took Bryshere to get his first haircut at the Philadelphia Hair Company. I thought that was the cutest thing. He had him sit still and behave, while the barber skillfully cut the best haircut for his tiny head. After his first time, I never took him to get a haircut while were in a relationship because it was their male bonding time. As we grew older, we eventually grew apart. He played a unique role in Bryshere's life when he needed him the most. But with us growing apart, we had to go our separate ways; it was for the best. Although I was heartbroken, our relationship ended on good terms. As fate would have it, he wouldn't be the first or the last man to break my heart.

**

Years later, my ex and I reconnected, yet again. He had since been married and now had a few children of his own. Once he started coming around again, he tried to show me how much he had changed. He wasn't rapping as much anymore, but he started an open mic event, which he held once a week. Many of the local artists frequented there because that was where they preferred to congregate. After working twelve-hour shifts at work, I drove directly to the venue to collect the admission fees at his events. Although I did it without being paid, that became one of my first jobs in the entertainment business. Eventually, we became engaged, and we moved in together. His children would often visit and play with mine as one big happy family. Bryshere gravitated toward him because they had something in common, music. He would be on the computer networking for his shows as my son sat next to him admiring every aspect of it. He and Bryshere would perform huddled around the computer in what is called a cypher, an informal gathering of rappers, beatboxers, and/or break-dancers in a circle, in order to jam musically together. They exchanged rhymes back and forth for hours until they finished, exploding into a burst of laughter. Ever since then, Bryshere was hooked on music.

I can recall like it was yesterday. One weekend, I was off of work, and Bryshere and my ex-fiancé's two sons came downstairs to the living room and performed for us in front of the mirror. They spent their time upstairs practicing and getting prepared like it was a real show. Sometimes, my ex-fiancé and I would join in with them. I would look around and feel like I finally had the family that I always wanted. I believed Bryshere felt the same way. He was elated, so I did my best to support my ex-fiancé any way I could. I wanted to help keep his music dream alive and give Bryshere happiness to hold on to for himself.

Even though my ex-fiancé didn't have much money, it was more satisfying to see our children happy together. We always had fun. During that time, Bryshere was exposed to the excitement of the music industry. For example, when we would go out as a family, Bryshere witnessed the amount of attention my ex-fiancé received from people who recognized him. I didn't want him to focus on the 'glitz and glam' solely. I wanted him to understand the music business in its entirety. He needed to embrace what he didn't love about it and still make it work for his benefit. I shared numerous stories with him to teach life lessons to prepare him for the industry better. The one story that was the most impactful was about my ex-fiancé. I let him know he was a one-hit wonder, and after his career had ended, it was difficult to reclaim his throne as a lyricist. My intention was not to scare Bryshere, but I needed him to know that the music business is a very unforgiving business. He was aware that, if he wanted it, he had to take the bad with the good and give it his all. I wanted him to be proactive and prepared for everything the business would deliver. I expressed to him that having talent was great, but not to rely on it; he needed to create a backup plan as well.

Once Bryshere turned twelve, my ex-fiancé and I had disagreements because of the atmosphere in the male-dominated entertainment world. He didn't want me speaking with other men in the industry. What he didn't realize was when I did converse with other guys, it was only to get their contact information for connections. I wasn't disrespectful, but he didn't view it that way. For some reason, he assumed I had ulterior motives. That notion remained in the forefront of his mind because he was always cheating. When handling business, I always remained professional, and most importantly I kept my focus. I wasn't going to stop networking with other men because he felt insecure. I networked with women as well, so I couldn't understand the issue he had. I was thinking about Bryshere's career, my daughter and a way to provide for my family.

As time went on, I noticed his infidelity was getting worse. One day, at his brother's wedding in Boston, we both decided we had enough after being off and on for two years. The relationship ended with an intense verbal dispute that progressed into a huge physical altercation. During the dispute, I asked him to leave. It was ironic to be celebrating someone else's union while experiencing the demise of our relationship.

My son didn't have many friends, so the relationship he had with his sons was a brother-like bond. I didn't realize the depth of how it affected him until we discussed it in his therapy sessions. I remember during one session; we were talking about school, his behavior and why it was so hard for him to listen to me. My son wouldn't initiate the conversation, so the therapist always had to ask him questions. I decided to talk about the breakup with my ex-fiancé. As soon as I began to speak about it, I could sense that he was bothered. Although he was sitting on the other end of the couch, I knew by his body language it was going to be a touchy subject to discuss.

As he sat there upset and stared straight ahead; the therapist asked if he was angry or sad about the breakup. He wouldn't open up at first, so he didn't respond. Then, I interjected and decided to reveal how I felt during the relationship and after it was over. I spoke about how much I cried and all the pain I endured. Speaking about the breakup in depth even caused me to become emotional during the session. By being vulnerable and truthful assured him it was okay to cry and share his feelings. That's when he admitted that he wished he had a father. He also felt like he had lost his brothers because when the relationship ended, he didn't see them anymore. My ex-fiancé promised he would always be there for him. I did my best to explain that the breakup didn't have anything to do with him. I furthered explained to him that sometimes even adults don't fully understand how to handle difficult issues and that's the reason we must rely on God. I let him know; we have to pray about everything and not worry about anything.

On the ride home, he was silent. He wouldn't say anything, and he barely moved. I turned on my gospel music so that I could create a calm atmosphere. I explained to him that just because someone doesn't live with you any longer, doesn't mean they don't love you anymore. I let him know how much his grandparents loved him and that Brianna and myself loved him deeply. I already knew he understood how much his family loved and supported him, but I gave him a little more reassurance. I wanted him to realize there were people around him that loved him, even if his father or my ex weren't there.

My daughter even noticed Bryshere was deeply hurt by my ex-fiancé's absence from our lives. Once again, he was disappointed by someone who said they would always be there for him. I could only imagine how he felt. They were extremely close during the year we lived together. Sometimes, when I reprimanded him in front of my ex-fiancé, he would come to his defense. He gave me better ways to address him so that things would operate smoother between us in the household. Sometimes, Bryshere would come into the room and want to talk to him and not me. Being that he didn't want his father in his life, I saw how ecstatic he was to have a male in the house other than himself. He was happy being able to talk to a man about some of his issues.

Although Bryshere didn't see how the breakup benefited him, it was for the best. Every decision I made was in consideration of my children. I didn't think of myself; they were always first in every strategic plan I had to move forward. I couldn't remain in toxic relationships that weren't beneficial to us as a family. Undoubtedly, I appreciate the role my ex-fiancé played the year he lived with us. It's not always about financial support. The time he took to have conversations with my son while he was there meant more to me than any amount of money in this world.

***

As I tried to be patient with being more knowledgeable about the different stages of this disorder, it seemed that his school decided just not to care at all. It went from receiving calls at home about his behavior, to the school immediately giving him detention. I objected to medicating him with Ritalin because I learned about the side effects it had on children. Whenever I took him to therapy, and they wanted to prescribe medication, I researched it first, then consented to the doctor's prescription. Usually, it was always the smallest dosage. As a mother, I didn't want my son to become addicted to anything, and I wanted to make sure we were going to see sustainable results.

The medication he was already taking gave him stomach pains. The first time I noticed, was when I cooked a large pot of spaghetti that should have lasted all three of us for at least two days. When I returned home that same day, it had all been eaten. That's when I knew something was wrong. After some research, I learned the medication wouldn't permit him to eat for approximately thirteen hours, and then he would come home and eat a large meal. Because of that, I researched, even more, medicine to avoid a recurrence. The therapist continued helping me to learn how to deal with him at each stage.

Even his lunch time was incorporated into the IEP. Since the medication suppressed his appetite, he wouldn't be hungry at the original time he was scheduled for lunch. Later on in the afternoon, he would be hungry but wasn't allowed to eat. I had to make sure they understood the reasoning behind his eating habits. It was overwhelming at times because I felt they thought I was making excuses for him. Making abrupt changes to his plan needed to be implemented immediately and with precision; timing was everything. The biggest challenge with the school was helping them understand that ADHD was a real condition. One teacher told me, "just let him be a boy." She dismissed his behavior as child's play.

As the therapy visits continued, the therapist stated it was possible the trauma I experienced from the abuse while I was pregnant, could have been the very cause of the ADHD. At that point, I knew I couldn't only educate myself; I had to educate Bryshere as well. I learned I couldn't ask him to do several things simultaneously. If I gave him a task of three things to do, he would only remember one. Before I finished my sentence, he would have already stopped listening to me. I thought when he wouldn't do everything I told him to do; he was just rebellious. That's when I learned I had to take it step by step and break things down for him. His medication was working for a while, and the teachers were able to deal with him slightly better. But when the medication would wear off, or his body developed a tolerance, it wouldn't work effectively anymore. He would begin acting out again, and we were back at square one. This time, when the phone calls came, I would sit at my work desk and cry. It was too much.

The feelings of being overwhelmed were practically my default. One day, as I drove along Kelly Drive, a popular four-mile stretch of road bordering the Schuylkill River in Philadelphia, the weight of exhaustion cloaked me. All throughout my day, Bryshere's teachers had called me for one thing or another. I pulled over to pray and think by the water. Before I could finish my prayer, I began to cry, and that cry soon turned into a wail as sadness overtook me. His problems at school were difficult enough to deal with on their own. But my stresses went beyond that. I was having trouble finding a babysitter that was the right match for him; one who could handle all that came along with having ADHD. Without one, I would not be able to work, and without work, I could not feed, clothe and shelter my children.

My life had gotten to the point where I honestly felt like no matter what I did; it wasn't enough for him. As I stood by the river crying, pouring my soul and troubles out for all to see, no one, out of all the people that filled the park that day, stopped to ask me if was okay. I was alone. I felt weak and helpless. I couldn't seem to do anything right when it came to my children. I fell to my knees, then cried out to God and asked Him to help me. I was on my knees for at least fifteen minutes, when I heard something tell me to pick my head up and think. And that's just what I did.

CHAPTER THREE

I was on a mission. I tried to put all the pieces together and keep going for the sake of my children. I just couldn't for the life of me understand why it was just me. Regardless of how hard I tried, I couldn't comprehend why Brianna's father wouldn't help me with her without me having to take him to court. Every thirty-one days, I had to enforce the court order because he refused to pay the mandated child support. If that wasn't exhausting enough, my daughter was upset with me because we weren't together. Bryshere's father wouldn't help me either. Yet I still pushed forward and continued working my jobs.

Balancing my family and my jobs was more than demanding, but I had goals. Going back to living with my parents wasn't an option, and there was no way I was going to let my family face homelessness. My objective was clear, and I concentrated on it at all times. In its due time, working two jobs afforded me the opportunity to purchase a new home in Overbrook, where I would raise my two children. My new home was unquestionably a blessing, but there were definitely adjustments.

I was no longer on welfare, and I was working hard to make sure our needs were met. Though working two jobs was financially beneficial, it did not come without sacrifice. Each moment that I spent at work was a moment that I wasn't with my children. They spent less and less time with me. I was acutely aware of this, and it took its emotional toll on me, but I had no choice. I needed the two incomes. Each day I would leave my home at six o'clock in the morning and wouldn't return until eleven-thirty or twelve at night. I was working sixty hours a week at the very least.

My father helped with my children at this point. When SEPTA, Southeastern Pennsylvania Transportation Authority, our primary public transit provider, went on strike, my father stepped in and helped with my children. The only thing that bothered me when he helped with Bryshere was that he always said that there wasn't anything wrong with him. That made me nervous. I later realized that he was approaching it from an 'old school' point of view. During his days as a kid, they weren't raised with the understanding of ADHD, so he didn't believe in the existence of disorders. I had to explain Bryshere's condition thoroughly so that he could grasp a better understanding. Once my father understood the issue, he helped even more. He never had women around my son. He kept his personal life very private and didn't have much time to himself because he was helping me so much.

I appreciated when my father attended our therapy sessions with us. He didn't come all the time, but he was present enough. He and my mother even attended sessions to explain to the therapist how they individually coped with Bryshere's ADHD. There were times my son spent more time with my father than he did with me. I knew it was because he was the one consistent male figure that he had in his life. Even though he came to therapy and understood some of the things that Bryshere was faced with; he had concerns with the medicine my son was taking. He spoke negatively about the medication because he was against him taking it. We disagreed when it came to that because there were times that I just didn't need the aggravation when it came to how I handled Bryshere's ADHD.

He was like my best friend, and he became the father figure that Bryshere needed. He taught him about being a young man and showed him things that I couldn't. My father had this watch that my son put on every time he took it off his wrist. I remember when I bought Bryshere a replica of it, he said, "Look, Pop Pop. I have my own watch; you can keep yours." And he loved trying on my dad's hats and shoes.

They were so much alike. I had a key to my father's place, and one day I walked in on them in the middle of an argument. I couldn't believe that he was arguing with a child. But there they were, two Sagittarius, accusing each other of cheating on the game. I saw my dad move the pieces on the board when Bryshere went to the bathroom. All I could do was laugh. I had no idea that his grandson would have limited time with him.

Thankfully, my father eventually moved in with me and helped me tremendously. It was a load off of my mind knowing that I had someone I trusted with my children; someone who would do things like taking them to and from school. Despite my busy schedule I still found time to be there for my children. It wasn't always the most typical of ways, nor was it always face to face, but I did what I could. While on my lunch break at my second job, I would call them and try to help them with their homework over the phone. Sometimes, I would wake up early at 4:30 a.m. to cook dinner for them before I left for work, and on Fridays and Saturdays, we would have pizza night. They were small gestures, but I did anything I could think of to let them know that they were always on my mind.

Shortly after, my father's doctor discovered he had cancer. Sadly, he died two days after the sixtieth birthday party I gave him. A few months later, I had a dream about him. In my dream, I was carrying his casket with other people. We were walking down the street, and we dropped the casket. The top of it opened, and he fell to the ground. He sat up in a sitting position in the middle of the street and proceeded to say, "You're going to be okay. Just always stay by your children's side. Bryshere will be fine." I wasn't afraid and embraced those words because I was so happy to hear his voice again.

When he passed away, that was the most detrimental time in my son's life. I thought I was taking it hard, but watching him go through that was very painful. He was doing well in school with the program that I'd put in place. When my dad passed away, I started getting calls again about him not doing his homework and projects. He missed his grandfather, and I knew that it was affecting him; it was affecting all of us. After my loss, I fell into a depression, but I was still able to function. I was in so much pain and took a leave of absence from work for four months. My bills fell behind, and I almost lost my house. I felt like both of my kids hated me and nobody wanted me. I was able to take care of my children and provide the things they needed, but mentally I wasn't there. All I did was lay in the bed when I came home.

I didn't eat or sleep much for weeks. I cried in my room and took Benadryl tablets to make me sleep. I started drinking Heineken beers; my life was spiraling out of control. I'm known in my family as being strong, so it was hard for people to see me at my lowest point. At the most unexpected times, life continued to throw hardballs at me. Sorrowfully, my parenting challenge was being strong and taking care of my children while I was grieving my father's death. There were days I went to work smiling like everything was fine, and then there were days I cried at work because the pain was too much to bear.

We were already dealing with issues when all of a sudden the water main broke in front of my house. I thought the City of Philadelphia was going to repair it because of the location of the damage. At the time, my insurance company sent me a letter stating that I had to pay $3,000 to have it repaired. I thought that my mortgage company was responsible for the bill because I paid everything through them. They didn't pay for it, and my policy was canceled two days before the issue could be resolved. Once that happened, I only had five days to get the situation rectified. When the main broke, the city threatened to turn my water off because water was running all day and night.

Before they interrupted my service, water ran down the street and mud piled up. My neighbors became frustrated and complained because it affected them as well. I didn't have the money to fix the problem. The city eventually disconnected the water supply, so we had to stay at a hotel for three weeks. Eventually, I applied for a personal loan to have the repairs completed. Although we were never homeless, there were many times I didn't know if I would lose our house or be able to afford any future emergency situations.

***

I wanted to get better, but I was still struggling mentally. It wasn't until my daughter came to me one day and said, "Mom, you're going to kill yourself." That's when I decided to do something. I prayed and spoke to my Pastor about fasting. I began practicing it on a consistent basis. I could see the change the next time I went through something difficult because I got through it without having a complete meltdown. I knew that I was slowly regaining my strength. I started going to therapy to further my steps toward healing.

I was stronger and had to be there for my children. Even when I think about how hard things were, I tried my best not to let my kids experience the struggles. They had cable in their rooms, and their beds weren't on the floor, which was common for children in our neighborhood. I spent every dime I had and didn't have just to give them the Christmas that they deserved. I didn't want them to be disappointed by not having gifts under the tree. When I was a child, I had gifts every year, so I wanted the same for them.

I found myself overcompensating for their missing fathers. I didn't want them to struggle and think that because their fathers weren't around, that's why things weren't right for us. I was in school and working sixteen hour days, which was rough. I knew that I had to sacrifice something. I had to get in my mind that you only get one chance with your children. I knew that I could go back to school at any time. I would attend for a year, then have to stop for a year because my kids weren't getting the best of me. People always stressed that I needed to finish for my children, but I knew they needed me more. It became a little embarrassing whenever I was asked about school because I had to put it on hold for a while. I did my best not to be affected because I knew what was best for my children and me.

I was dealing with a lot of hurtful things that people said about me. My family said things like I couldn't keep a man. But I sacrificed being in a relationship because I felt most men probably couldn't deal with Bryshere's disorder and episodes. Because of that, I believed I could only date when his condition was under control. Being a positive influence in my children's lives was more important to me than anything else. I may not have been able to raise him to be a man, but I knew I could raise him to be a gentleman.

I recall teaching him to open doors for females. I took my children to the mall, and I never touched a door. When we entered the elevator, I told him always to let the ladies get on first. One time we were on the elevator, and we stood behind an older woman. When the doors opened, he rushed passed her just to beat her to the door; so he could open it. The woman was so appreciative and kept praising him for his manners. It made him very proud to be acknowledged for doing a good deed. When I saw him display those acts of kindness, I knew that I was doing my best. I just keep praying and asking God to give me the strength I needed always to put my children first, just like my father told me to do.

Along with buying a new house, came an abundance of bills. In addition to furnishing my home, I was now responsible for paying a monthly mortgage and utilities. I was eternally grateful for my new home and was well aware of what owning a home entailed; it was just frustrating to have worked so hard to move up, only to struggle more than I had before. The bills seemed insurmountable. I wasn't used to having a four hundred dollar gas bill. Shut off notices began to appear and I eventually maxed out all my credit cards.

One day, while at work, I received a phone call from the credit card company informing me that they were going to garnish my wages until the card account was paid down. I felt helpless. I pleaded with them not to take my money. Although I knew the money was rightfully theirs, I needed my wages. I cried out to God asking, *What did I do wrong? I just wanted to put my children in a better circumstance.*

Thankfully, I was able to make payment arrangements with that particular card company and others, but I had to work more than I already was to meet my obligations. Naturally, this meant more time away from my children. I hated that I wasn't able to physically sit with them and help with their homework. It bothered me deeply. The more I worked, the more I noticed how my children felt about me not being around.

Almost imperceptibly at first, their behavior would change. The calls home from Bryshere's school were more common, and the topics of discussion worsened. My daughter had behavioral issues as well. Looking back, I can see how they felt that I could have been more nurturing to them, but they needed more than I was able to give. And not because I chose to not spend time with them, or because I felt they weren't deserving of my time, but because I had a difficult choice to make. When it came down to choosing between having free time or providing food, shelter and other necessities for my children; I chose the latter. I did the best I could with the free time I did have. If I only had two hours to spend with them, then I made sure that every second of our time together counted. There were many nights that I would lay in bed and cry. The heaviness of a hard life weighed upon me. At times I felt that it was too much to withstand, but I would never let my children see me cry. I had to learn how to cope and deal without them seeing me break.

**

The day I graduated from The Community College of Philadelphia, my parents, siblings, and children were all in attendance. That morning, my kids greeted me with hugs and kisses, and told me they loved me. They watched me put on my cap and gown. When they left my bedroom, I cried tears of joy. I had temporarily put my dreams aside to make a better life for them, and now they saw me accomplish a primary goal. My two-year Associate's degree in general studies took eight years to obtain. I felt blessed that I could show them that you can still achieve your goals despite your age.

I remember the days before my exams; I spent the entire time studying in the library. As a result, Bryshere was upset and gave me the silent treatment because I spent more time in the library than at home. After I finished studying and came home, his room door would be closed signifying he didn't want to speak. When I peeked my head in to greet him, he would just brush me off with a simple wave. I could feel his energy and knew I had to salvage our relationship. I completely understood his frustrations but was determined to make him feel better. He would be playing his video game, and I would try to talk to him. He would interrupt me and say, "I'm playing my game right now. Can you come back later?" My feelings were deeply hurt, but I knew I was doing the right thing by attending college. I didn't want my children to feel unloved, so I kept encouraging and motivating myself to keep going.

After graduating, I wanted to attend nursing school for the next chapter of my life. I decided to attend but had to re-take several classes because I took some time away from classes. Some of the pre-requisite courses I had previously taken expired because of not being enrolled. It took me two years to complete four classes. At that time, I entered another nursing program at Widener

University. I progressed to my third year but didn't pass my last class. I failed for the second time, and I was extremely discouraged. I didn't even know how to face my children. Here I was pushing them to follow their dreams, and I could barely pass a few courses. I knew I could compete academically, but I didn't have enough time to dedicate to my studies. I didn't want my children to feel unloved again. Eventually, I withdrew from school and took a four-year hiatus.

**

After years passed, I sat my children and told them the plan I had in mind. I decided to re-enroll in school, and let them know, once I became a nurse, I would only have to work three days a week instead of seven. This time, I advanced to my third semester. When I received grades of A's and B's, I would tape the paper to their bedroom doors for motivation. It was my way of trying to encourage them. One time, Bryshere and I had a competition. I brought home an A paper and told him if he brought home an A, I would purchase a new video game. He worked hard and delivered on his promise. He earned an A in reading, and I was so proud. If Brianna earned A's, I took her shopping or gave her money to buy whatever she wanted. It felt good knowing my entire family was attending school. There were times we'd all study together in the living room. I appreciated this family time since we didn't have much of it during my days in school. Studying as a family helped him stay focused. To avoid any distractions, I powered off all electronics, put the phones upstairs and the dog in the basement. As much as I tried to minimize the distractions, Bryshere would still find a reason to get up and move around.

***

Although I had to limit the number of hours I worked, I received a stipend because I was enrolled in school. I used those funds to contribute to the household bills. Then, there were other expenses I had to account for, such as his sports uniforms. It seemed like that extra expense would always come at the worst time. But I didn't take anything away from him that kept him focused. Usually, I worked sixty hours a week, and I lowered my hours to forty-eight hours a week. I was already struggling financially with the overtime I was working, and then lost forty percent of my bi-weekly gross. To watch my income drop drastically was devastating. The kids noticed the change as well because I had to limit some of their activities and luxuries. Being able to watch cable was one of those luxuries, but I had to struggle to keep that from being disconnected. That was a needed benefit for Bryshere to give him some form of entertainment.

I had to be strategic with the way in which I purchased food. The food had to last for days at a time, so I cooked spaghetti and chicken wings often. I noticed how my children adjusted to whatever changes occurred.

There were many times I had to do what I had to do to survive, so they had to adjust quickly. They didn't always understand, but they adjusted. Many times, I went to work and didn't have lunch, so they didn't suffer. At work, potlucks, a gathering where each guest contributes a dish of food, often homemade, to be shared, were a Sunday tradition. I took full advantage of the opportunity to get a diverse meal for my children. Even though times became so hard, I couldn't afford to bring food. One nurse didn't mind and told me to help myself to the multitude of platters available. I was elated. Another nurse did mind, so sadly I was unable to get a plate. I remember going to the bathroom and crying. No one knew my situation, and because people recognized I was well put together, they had no idea I was struggling financially. I was too embarrassed, so I never mentioned that I didn't have money for lunch or that I didn't eat all day. Being placed in that situation taught me that you never know what someone is going through, so I vowed from that day forward to never place judgment upon anyone.

There was much financial stress during that time. The co-pays that I had for his therapy and medications were expensive, and I always included those in the budget. His medicine and therapy combined were one hundred thirty dollars per month. To me, that was an exorbitant amount to add to my already existing bills. The amount needed each month increased, but my income decreased; there was a huge imbalance. When times were rough financially, I felt like things were completely out of control. Being able to pay the bills provided me with a piece of mind, so when I couldn't, I was overwhelmed. There were so many other things I couldn't do; this compounded my depression.

I hated that my children had to experience those difficult times, but I knew I was working as hard as I possibly could. As long as they had food and a roof over their heads, I knew we could overcome anything. Then one day, I asked myself, *Would having more money change my situation?* I had to face my reality. I realized, even with better finances, my child was dealing with a disorder that was supposedly incurable. Maybe having more money would've permitted me to be home more, but it didn't guarantee his condition would be more tolerable. Truthfully, I knew deep down inside; more money only meant a much-needed vacation, and a chance to take my children places they had never been. It surely didn't constitute my son would be freed from the shackles of his ADHD.

***

My battle with his disorder was never-ending, so once again my education would have to wait. My parents couldn't handle helping out with Bryshere, so I joined an ADHD support group. Depending on my schedule, I attended twice a month. The group was composed primarily of single parents. I may have seen only one father, and the others in attendance were all women. One of the things I remembered most, was how to make your other children feel loved and not ignored. Most children with the disorder required the majority of your attention, so it was key be attentive to your child.

As parents, we shared our stories and experiences. One mother told me a heartbreaking story about her daughter who was stealing. She was forced to put locks on her doors, and it became difficult to keep her in the household. She loved her daughter but was afraid her actions would influence the other children. So, she battled whether or not to put her in foster care. Another parent spoke about her son who fraternized with the wrong crowd. There were multiple home invasions in her neighborhood, and all the houses were robbed except hers. She suspected her son and his friends were involved, but she didn't have solid proof. She did all she could to prevent him from being with them, but to no avail.

Statistics show it is normal for people with ADHD to engage in criminal activity. Individuals with the condition are twice as likely to commit crimes and commit three times as many offenses as those without the disorder. They are more susceptible to problematic drug use and more likely to attempt suicide. This made me more aware of Bryshere and his behavior. When he was around people that I felt weren't conducting themselves in a positive manner, I would address it immediately. Even the principal at his school knew I was a dedicated parent, so she kept a close eye on him. As he furthered himself in school, the principal provided additional support, such as speaking with him when he had trouble completing his assignments in class. On the rare occasions I had off from work, I visited the school and conversed with the faculty about providing my assistance to make the school environment better. I knew it required teamwork, so I was open to suggestions and new strategies to implement. I needed them to know I was doing everything in my power to help the situation.

When he was eleven, he received an MVP award in football. When he accepted it, he let everyone in attendance know that he was grateful that I took care of him. I was very proud of him receiving an award and staying focused on the sport that he loved. I knew my son played well, but he was more talented than I realized. I remember he was playing in an away game and the coach from the other team shouted, "Get number twenty-two! Make sure you watch out for him!" I was shocked because hearing that his athleticism threatened the other team made me realize he had talent. At that moment, I knew he had worked very hard to prove himself on the field.

I began to see some improvements in school, while our life at home became more challenging. He disliked people being in his personal space, so physically disciplining him was not an option. I had to explain to his teachers, it was imperative they didn't approach him aggressively or invade his personal space in any way. He felt threatened in those types of situations, so I was trying to protect him as well as the staff. People didn't always understand it was mandatory to deal with him differently. For some, it was hard to comprehend something as minuscule as their approach made a difference in whether they had a good or bad day with Bryshere.

I was mentally and emotionally exhausted. Someone wasn't always available for Bryshere to visit so I could have a break. I began thinking about what I needed to make this work differently. The medication he was prescribed was slowly being ineffective, and I couldn't increase the dosage. Although he struggled with controlling his behavior, I hated watching him deal with the side effects of his medicine, which sometimes included stomach pains or burning eyes. It also made him feel sluggish. I didn't want him to be like a zombie, so he was prescribed a low dosage. It was hard trying to discipline him because he didn't comprehend why he was being punished. As an alternative, I took away his video games and prevented him from playing in his football games. It was painful watching him sit on the bench while other kids participated. I enjoyed watching him play, so it was like punishing myself when he was confined to the sideline.

By the time he was a pre-teen, he was even more rebellious. A typical day for us would begin with a light breakfast that consisted of toast, fruit, and a glass of orange juice. Then, I gave him his medicine and sent him to school. After a while, I noticed he was losing weight. I was quite concerned, so I ceased giving him the medication to determine if it was the cause. I switched his medicine as much as the doctor permitted to find the appropriate one for him. Only the teachers knew about his condition, so to avoid being teased by his classmates I didn't allow him to take his medication at school.

During this time, it felt like I was carrying both our pain. Much of mine stemmed from wanting his father to be in his life and not understanding how to deal with his disorder. I was also frustrated because I followed the proper steps but still felt like I was failing. Brianna's father was partially in her life until he was incarcerated, but Bryshere's father didn't play an active role in his life at all. I began noticing a change in my daughter's behavior. She disliked how I treated Bryshere. She felt that I favored him because I talked to him instead of physically disciplining him when he did something wrong. Deep inside, I was sympathetic because he didn't have a male figure around. I know many women believe they can be a mother and father, but there are some male things that a woman just can't do.

As time went on, his behavior shifted again. This time it escalated to him running away from home. There was an incident where he and his sister were home alone because they were of responsible ages. Since Brianna was the oldest, I left her in charge to ensure the household was in an order similar to how I maintained it. They began to dispute so severely, that she repeatedly called me at work to mediate. I had to remain calm and let him know his sister was merely enforcing rules by my instruction. Once I had his attention, I continued with what I needed for him to complete before I arrived home.

When I arrived, I had to verbally discipline him, which caused him to become so upset, he punched holes in the wall. Then, it was later revealed he crept out the house when I was asleep. I set my alarm clock to conduct random house checks in the middle of the night because his behavior was so unstable. When the alarm sounded, I checked his room first and noticed he wasn't there. I discussed the situation with him later on and told him I hoped it was an isolated incident. I further let him know, if it happened again, I would be forced to send him away to a facility.

He was adamant about not being sent away. I firmly believe, in the back of his mind he felt there was truth behind my words, so he became frightened and ran away. The police found him at one of his friend's house and returned him back home. He felt that if I sent him away, it was a sign I didn't love him anymore. He didn't understand that I was only trying to protect him. Instead, he interpreted sending him away meant I could spend more time with Brianna. He didn't understand that I wanted to save him from making the wrong decisions that could cost him his life. I knew I wasn't only overprotective because of his disorder. He was a young black male living in America - he was born with two strikes against him. His ADHD compelled me to be more protective because I knew his condition could cause the third strike.

There were times I wished I was married, not only because I wanted a companion and desired to be loved, but frankly I also needed help. I would find myself growing weary with my circumstances. I covered the pain and anger with partying in attempts to bring my spirits up. There were times when I had to make the decision between buying food or paying the bills. I always chose to have food for my children to eat. As far as the bills were concerned, I had no other choice but to make yet another payment arrangement. To say that it was embarrassing is an understatement, but embarrassment isn't fatal, and I had to find a way to survive.

The more I thought about my situation in life; I wondered if somewhere along the way, I skipped a necessary step. Nothing was going as I envisioned it. I was a mother of two, struggling to make ends meet. I had a long list of daily worries from finance to being a great parent. Added to those problems were my concerns with Bryshere's ADHD. There were times that I felt like I wasn't going to make it through. I was burning the candle at both ends and finding myself feeling burned out. To make matters worse, I also began to feel like I was burning out those who were helping me. My mother had two children of her own to raise, but she still watched mine. Of course, she never complained.

During tough times, it wasn't always easy to find the support that I needed from my friends. When I had my children, most of my other friends weren't parents. While I never had the expectation that their lives would revolve around me because I made a choice to become a parent, it still felt like I had lost a lot of friends. I now had responsibilities that they didn't, and I was always working. Further complicating matters was that when I was free to hang out with them, there was no guarantee that someone would be available to watch my children. It was but by the grace of God that I had two wonderful friends by my side.

My friend, Sonji, from college, was just as great as my mother when it came to offering her assistance. She had four children of her own, but never hesitated to watch Bryshere and Brianna; sometimes she would watch them for an entire weekend. Her husband, Barrett, who was a professional football player, was a positive male role model for my children. On those occasions where I needed a release, he would watch all of the children so that my best friend and I could go out and enjoy ourselves. He would take them to the movies, introduce them to new things and afford them the opportunity to experience life in an atmosphere different than the one they were used to.

Over the summer, Bryshere and Brianna would stay with my best friend and her husband for weeks, which allowed me to put in more hours at work. I would work a shift from 7:00 a.m. to 3:00 p.m., come home, rest for a bit and return to work at 11:00 p.m. to get off at 3:00 p.m. the next day. I was exhausted, and it grew harder and harder to get out of bed each morning; especially if I worked a double shift the night before. My doubles were sixteen hours, and on some occasions, I would work twenty hours a day. I did this by working at two different hospitals that were directly across from each other. There were times that I found myself bouncing from one hospital to the other to work as many hours and get as much overtime as possible.

Luckily, I had my best friend Lisa, whom I have been friends with for over thirty years. She has supported me and stood by my side through thick and thin. If there were ever a time that I didn't have a babysitter, whether it was for work or a little free time to myself, Lisa would graciously invite my children over and watch them for me. She is a blessing. Her generous nature makes her understanding and patient with my son. Lisa would even go so far as to develop strategies to help him cope with his ADHD. On the days where a babysitter wasn't necessary, and I was overwhelmed by all the encompassed me, she came to my home and pray with me. There were many nights that she stayed by my side as I cried myself to sleep. More than anything I genuinely appreciated that she never judged me or my situation, and she always encouraged me to keep going.

Lisa is a trusted confidant to both my children and me. If my daughter felt there was something that she didn't want to confide in me, she would speak in confidence to her. When I had reached my tipping point and was seriously considering sending my son to an institution that could better serve his needs, it was Lisa who remained hopeful and helped me to see the positive side of staying strong and not giving up. On the two occasions that Brianna ran away, it was Lisa who helped me look for her.

While Lisa never judged, there was occasional frustration on my part because she and I had different methods of parenting and we didn't always agree. She expressed to me that she didn't think I needed to work as often or that I should avoid dating. Lisa is my best friend, and I love her with all of my heart. But at that time, our situations were so entirely different, so I felt she couldn't possibly fully understand the magnitude of what I was experiencing. I wasn't ever upset when she voiced her opinions. How could I have been when it was me who had invited her into the details of my life? Besides, I knew that her opinions came from a place of love. She is the one real friend that stuck by me when everyone else didn't care one way or the other. She always has my back, even when I couldn't necessarily see it.

CHAPTER FOUR

As Brianna grew older, she began to take issue with the special attention that, from her perception, I showed Bryshere. She felt that my attention and focus was predominately on him; and that the time I spent with him, championing for him or researching his ADHD was a clear indication that I loved him more than I did her. In her mind, I wasn't as concerned with her or her needs. I can still perfectly remember the day she came to me and asked, "Do you love him more than me?"

When Brianna first posed this question to me, I was blown away. It was if I could physically feel my heart shatter into a million pieces. It hurt me to think that for a second she could think I loved her any less. But as we spoke, I began to understand her feelings, regardless of how amiss they were. Admittedly, because of his ADHD diagnosis, I disciplined Bryshere and Brianna differently; however, where I saw compassion for him she saw favoritism. She was the oldest sibling; therefore, I naturally expected her to help me out by assisting him with his chores. In frustration, she would come to say things such as "I'm not his mother." Her words stung. Of course, I knew she wasn't his mother, but she played an integral part in allowing me to work outside of the home. With a lump in my throat, I explained to her that the three of us were a team, and I dealt with his disorder the way I did to make things better for all of us. It was never to treat her worse than him, make her feel excluded or as if I didn't love her.

The manner in which I disciplined Bryshere and my hesitation to do so stemmed from my attempts to avoid the tantrums and the fighting that were corollary with his condition. Brianna came to recognize the differences in my disciplinary style between the two of them and soon challenged me on it. Once, when she was punished for not submitting a homework assignment, she said to me, "You don't discipline Bryshere. I didn't do my homework because I'm tired." Deep down I knew she had a point, and although I understood her frustration, I still disciplined her. Her response was a tantrum of her own. She went up to her room, threw things around and continuously opened and slammed her door. My response was to take her door off of the hinges until she learned some respect. But I knew she was more hurt than anything and decided that it was time to sit her down to have an open and frank discussion.

As she sat patiently across from me full of frustration and a bit of resentment, I explained to her that I wasn't picking on her and that I did care for her more than she could ever know. I told her how beautiful she was and how proud she made me on a daily basis. I asked her to try to understand that Bryshere had challenges that she didn't. While none of this was of her doing, I requested that she have a little patience with me and the way I dealt with the two of them. It was probably a lot to ask emotionally of her considering she was dealing with, not only a disconnect between her and I because of my attentiveness to Bryshere, but also the fact that her father had another family.

We hadn't been together since she was born. And like many young girls who need their fathers, she had questions. She began questioning why he and I weren't together. With everything that was happening, she tried to understand, but she couldn't help but develop resentment toward Bryshere.

Still, Brianna began to lash out. She attempted to run away twice and became involved with a boyfriend that she knew did not have my approval. There were times that I would have to leave work to look for her after I received a call from her school informing me that she had not shown up that day. She was getting into fights, and her grades were dropping. One night, she didn't come home. I knew where she was and called the cops to accompany me to her boyfriend's house. When we arrived, no one opened the door. Through the closed door, I told his mother that I was going to stay parked outside her home until Brianna came outside. Eventually, they sent her home. Other times, his mother lied and said

Brianna wasn't at her house, even though I knew she was. From that moment, I made sure that I gathered all of the details of where Brianna was going and who she would be with; just in case I had to show up on someone's doorstep to get her.

It was a difficult period, to say the least, and although I wished it were easier, I continued to understand her frustration. I just wanted her to realize that she could vent her frustrations without getting caught up in unsafe situations on the streets of Philadelphia. And I most certainly didn't view spending the night at her boyfriend's house as a viable option because I did not want her to become a teenage mother. Though the reasoning behind their behavior was different, I dealt with Brianna running off the same way I handled it when Bryshere did the same. I made sure they understood the consequences and everything that could go awry if I couldn't get to them.

I needed them to know that I loved them will all of my heart, but everything I did out of love wasn't always going to feel good to them. Some of it would feel like I was unfair or that I didn't understand them, but hopefully, they could see that I was showing my love for them by protecting them. I sacrificed a lot to make sure that they knew they were first, and even though they couldn't always see it, there wasn't anything I wouldn't do to protect them.

I started taking Bryshere to my mother's so that Brianna and I could have a girls' day from time to time. We would go to the mall, shop a bit and get manicures and pedicures. There were other times that we just hung out with each other. We would sit, have lunch, and talk about boys and life. I soon realized after a few of our girls' day, that my time was all she wanted. I sincerely appreciated that I didn't have to spend money on her for her to be happy; she was content with having my attention. It was during one of our outings that she revealed to me that she sometimes felt alone and often depressed. It saddened me to learn that Brianna was dealing with so much darkness and I had failed to realize it.

Over the course of our conversations, I also found out that Bryshere was teasing her. He would throw it in her face that I spent more time with him than her, and say things like "That's why mommy loves me more than you." When she spoke these words, the correlation between Brianna's initial question and Bryshere's statement hit me like a lightning bolt. His words, although meant as a tease, hit upon insecurities that she was already having. I sat both of them down and explained to them that I loved them equally and the time I spent with each of them did not correspond with how much I loved them. There had been times in Bryshere's life where he was teased for things beyond his control, and he knew it didn't feel good. I asked him to remember that feeling the next time he was tempted to hurt his sister's feelings intentionally.

One day, I asked Brianna what she liked about her brother to ease the tension between them. She said he's funny and he was always acting like a clown. I asked him the same question, and he told me she protected him and always had his back. I then asked what they didn't like about the other. He hated that she wouldn't let him into her room. Brianna hated that he would go into her room and take her large, gold rope chain to pretend that he was Run DMC. She didn't like that he was unorganized and all over the place. Her main point was that he would always mess up a new dish directly after she'd finished washing all of them. After many conversations, the two began to understand the other's side a little better. She agreed that Bryshere could wear her chain as long as he asked first and he realized that he had been inconsiderate with the dishes.

Even with Brianna's frustration with Bryshere, she was his fiercest protector. She would regularly be upset with me when he was disciplined with a spanking. If she sensed that I was going to spank him, she would place herself in our vicinity in the hopes that her presence would keep me from disciplining him. On one particular occasion, as I was in his room about to discipline him, I turned to see Brianna standing behind me and asked her what she was doing. Her reply was, "I just heard a lot of noise, and I wanted to make sure everything was okay." I stared at her for a moment and then sent her back to her room.

After things had calmed down, I called Brianna down to the dining room and had a discussion with her regarding why she felt she needed to come into his room that day. I explained to her that I would never, under any circumstance, abuse her brother, but there are times that he may need to be disciplined by a spanking. She earnestly replied that she didn't think it was working and that I was exhausting myself because he was still doing what he wanted. Initially, I was offended, but then I realized that she was right.

For as much as they had their problems, Brianna's watchful eye over Bryshere extended beyond the confines of our home. She attended the same school as her brother for two years, and she saw a lot more than I did. In truth, I learned a lot of what was really going on at the school from her. She witnessed how some teachers would treat him, and she didn't like it. Some teachers would go far as speaking badly about her brother, sometimes in front of the students. Which would as expected led to tension between him and the other children, especially when they would mention his ADHD. Other teachers used her to calm Bryshere down whenever he would act out. Her general feeling was that on most occasions, the teachers weren't helping him. They were just trying to get rid of him. Instead of helping him work through his problems, they chose to stick him in detention. Brianna tried her best to help him avoid problems by speaking to him and explaining that it would be less contentious if he just did as the teacher asked him.

I was glad that she understood that Bryshere wasn't always the problem. In some instances, it was a matter of the teachers dealing with him inappropriately. One of his biggest problems was boredom. He was a very bright child, but the fact of the matter was he got bored easily. His behavior had nothing to do with intelligence. When he was in third grade, he was at a fifth-grade reading level.

It was a different experience for Brianna altogether when it came to Bryshere's career. Being as she was a young lady and the studios were filled with nothing but men, I kept her away from his recording sessions. Most of the time, Brianna would be at my mother's house while Bryshere and I worked towards forwarding his career. As he found more success, I began to see old feelings resurface. She began to feel once again that he was getting more attention than she was. It wasn't in anything she said, but it was definitely in her actions. Admittedly, between his practices and his shows I was with him quite often. There were instances when my time with Bryshere affected her directly. Because I arrived home so late, she did too being as she had to wait until I picked her up from my mother's house. By the time we all got home, we were tired, and her homework suffered.

As Brianna's grades began to reflect the reduced time spent on homework, I asked her why she never asked for help with her assignment. But it dawned me that she didn't need help, she needed my attention.

I once again found myself in the position of having more to do than I had time, and once again it wasn't Brianna's fault. I asked her to support her brother and to try to view his burgeoning career in rap as a good thing. He finally had something that helped him focus and calmed him down. When he was performing, or in the studio, his ADHD was all but nonexistent. I implored her to appreciate that anything that focused him and gave a positive outlet for his energy was worth supporting. While all that was one hundred percent accurate, she felt that I always supported him in his endeavors, but I neglected to push her to do anything great. She pointed to the example that I never accompanied her to dance class, yet I always went with Bryshere to the clubs. I could see where she may have felt bad about it, but I explained to her that I had no other choice but to go with him to the clubs because he was underage and couldn't be there alone, even if it was to perform.

As Bryshere became busier, Brianna had to hold her own at home and started working just as much as I did. As a result, her absences from Bryshere's performances increased. There were times I wished she could've attended more of his shows to demonstrate just how much she supported him, but as someone who often worked long hours, I understood.

Much to Bryshere's pleasure, one of his sisters from his father's side, would come to many of his shows. He would ask why one of his other sisters was able to come, but not Brianna. Thankfully, Brianna was eventually able to come to a few of his shows. However, it didn't change the feeling that there always seemed to be a disconnect between the three of us. We were never on the same page, despite what was going on.

As Bryshere grew into his teenage years, when he was upset with me, he would rely on his sister. He would also talk about girls and other things that he didn't want to discuss with me. It made me proud and happy to see them building a connection, even if I wasn't always a part of it.

When Bryshere first came into his stardom, he took me to all of the awards shows with him. Due to her work schedule, Brianna hasn't had the experience as of yet, but last year, he flew my now deceased sister out to the BET Awards. She was stricken with cancer, and he really wanted to give her the experience of attending an award show with him. When they arrived, he gave her a big hug and said, "You finally made it here with me." She had a ball that night. She got a chance to see what his life was like as a celebrity and also to be a part of it. It was a sight to behold, and I hope that one day I will be able to see Brianna with her brother on the red carpet. I pray that at some point, she understands that my love for her is unconditional, even if she didn't fully get it when she was younger. I know that I did my best and even when I felt like I had failed. I know that the day will come when they both appreciate my sacrifices and how hard I worked to give us a better life.

CHAPTER FIVE

Romantic relationships are nothing new to me. I've dated and even been engaged, but it doesn't change the fact that dating with children brings about a unique set of challenges. I wasn't ready to share with everyone that my son had ADHD and harbored a lot of embarrassment when outsiders peered into my word of living with a child with a disorder. I also didn't want my children to develop an attachment and run the risk of them getting hurt if the relationship didn't work out.

Honestly, I was much more concerned with Bryshere developing an attachment than Brianna because she had her father in her life. As time gradually passed, there was a gentleman that I dated who I felt I could introduce to my children. I started off slowly by inviting him over for dinner. After introducing him as a good friend of mine, I watched intently as he interacted and engaged with Brianna and Bryshere. Brianna asked a lot of questions, but the children seemed to like him, and overall everything went well.

After the success of the first dinner, I began to invite my gentleman friend over a little more frequently. Being as things were going well between us, I began to let him spend the night under the condition that Bryshere and Brianna did not know. This was when they were much younger, and their bedtimes were around eight o'clock. For that reason, invited him over around ten and made sure that he left around five o'clock the next morning before they woke up.

This was our routine for a while before we both made the decision that it was time to go full-steam ahead with our relationship. The relationship had lasted for about two years before we decided it was best to part ways. He had begun to drink more, and sometimes our arguments lead to his aggressive behavior. Because of my past experiences, I wasn't comfortable with that. I was scared that our arguments would turn into physical altercations, so we both agreed that we should move on.

Although a physical threat never happened, I couldn't take the risk. Not only for my safety, but for the mental well-being of my children. There was a time when my ex-fiancé and I became embroiled in a heated argument. Bryshere burst into the room thinking that my ex-fiancé was harming me. I can still see the anger on his face as he surveyed the situation. This was new to him, even though it wasn't to me. He had never seen his father hit me and I didn't want him ever to have the experience of seeing me in that type of circumstance. He had also never seen me that vulnerable, and I worried that he would think less of me for allowing my ex-fiancé to behave that way towards me. After that incident, I could sense Bryshere withdrawing from me. I had him speak to the therapist about it because I figured that he might not want to share his feelings on this particular subject with me.

Because of the way my romantic relationship affected him, I made the conscious choice to be celibate and remain single. To numb the pain of being lonely, I threw myself into my work and taking care of my children. I wanted to date, but my desire was unmatched by obligations to my family. Finding happiness was second to making sure that my space was protected for my children's sake.

As in most situations, I regularly received advice from well-meaning, but unknowing outsiders. They would tell me that I needed to find a man for my son because he didn't need to be in the house with just women. But no one offering their advice took the time the look at the deeper issue. When things went wrong in my relationships, I had to pick up the pieces for three people, not just for myself. I had to build my strength and show people that God would take care of anything that I couldn't. Fasting and prayer had become second nature to me at this stage in my life. I was crying out to God to help me deal with the loneliness that wretched my heart each night. I was stressed, and it was becoming unhealthy. That's when it dawned on me that I had to get to know myself before I attempted to know anyone else. This realization made me take a few steps back, and I started to figure out both what I wanted and what I needed.

It wasn't an easy task by any stretch of the imagination. I can recall taking my children to the movies and seeing happy couples. That would stir the feeling that something was missing. One night, while we were in public, Bryshere turned to me and said, "I wish I had a dad." It was if I were made of glass and his words rained on me with the weight of a thousand hammers. They broke me. My heart wept. His words, although innocent enough to him, made me feel like everything I had done was wrong because I didn't choose the best fathers for my children. To this day, I am haunted by that feeling, and I wholeheartedly believe that many of their issues stem from not having their fathers around full-time. To ensure that my romantic choices never caused them any more undue pain I vowed that whenever I was ready to resume dating, whoever I chose would have to be perfect for all of us.

Bryshere's ADHD had to be taken into consideration when I selected my mate. Most people who date someone with children expect for there to be some challenges, but to deal with two kids, and one with a disorder was a lot. There would be times when I felt like I had an angel on one shoulder telling me that I was making the right decision by waiting. And on the other shoulder, a devil was telling me to forget about the way my kids would feel and to do what made me happy. In the midst of all this, I had to deal with my family not agreeing with the way I raised my children. When I took my daughter's father to court, I received a lot of flack about it. I felt like he was raising another family. So, why couldn't he take care of his daughter? Some even felt that I was being immature. Frankly, I didn't understand their need to address the situation in the least considering I wasn't asking them to contribute to the care of my children. As far as Bryshere's father was concerned, I had never received child support and taking him to court was a waste of time.

I must admit though, that all of the trials showed me exactly what I was not willing to accept in a relationship. I had no patience for a man who had children and opted not to take care of them. Second to this were aggressive guys. Overly aggressive behavior was an automatic deal breaker and cause for me to exit immediately. I didn't think that my criteria for dating were outlandish or too stringent in any way. However, I did realize that outside of these two requisites I could no longer base all of my interactions with men off of my past; it wasn't fair to them. I had to accept that, like me, men were human and imperfect. Therefore, I needed to learn to lend some grace and acknowledge that there are times that men need the same understanding and patience that I do.

While I wasn't going to automatically be with just anyone to appease my loneliness or the whispers of those around me, my biggest prayers during Christmas were that God would send Bryshere a father, and that my circumstance would allow me to be home more. No matter how much it hurt my son not to have his father around, I had to maintain my integrity when choosing a mate. I needed to wait for God to send me the right man.

I also wanted Bryshere to have a healthy image of his mother. What would it look like if I was always hanging onto somebody new and couldn't control myself when it came to men? Not to mention, I had to be careful of the example I was setting for Brianna. I couldn't be one of those mothers that told their children to 'do as I say and not as I do.' I had to be what I wanted to see in them, even if it meant sacrificing my happiness to make sure they were surrounded by positive behavior.

CHAPTER SIX

Raising my children in West Philadelphia was a huge challenge and sacrifice. Considered one of the city's roughest neighborhoods, there were many schools in our district on the city's most dangerous list. It was his junior high school years that we were mostly affected by the educational limitations. The school he attended ended at the eighth grade, so I had to send him to another school. When he had his eighth-grade dance, the principal didn't want him to attend. I didn't want to tell him that one of the reasons was because he was disruptive in class. I pleaded with the principal to give him another chance. She eventually consented, and he enjoyed himself.

A few months later, when it was time for him to graduate, we had the same problem. He was rehearsing and all, but then I received a call from the principal. She said he couldn't walk in the ceremony because he was misbehaving and refused to listen to her. The day of graduation, he was at home in his room very upset. I tried to help him understand that at least he was promoted to the next grade. I also wanted him to take responsibility for his behavior. I was proud that he passed his grade, so I took him out to dinner and let him take pictures in his cap and gown. He was excited about that, but I made him promise that he would walk in his high school graduation.

Bryshere didn't want to attend a school that didn't have a football team, Many of the ones that had a team were known for violence. I thoroughly researched each school he considered for its football program. Even though he had a friend that died from a football related accident; it didn't deter him. They were at practice, and two of the kids tackled each other. They must've collided too hard because he died on the field. My son was sad but still wanted to attend the funeral services to pay his respects. A short time afterward, he began to change in a positive way. He apologized for his behavior and started to adhere to the things I said for a while.

After my research, I concluded that the schools located in my neighborhood weren't a good fit for Bryshere. On my days off from work, I visited each school before classes commenced and after classes ended, to get a feel for the environment. Students were prone to getting into trouble before and after school, and I didn't want that for my son.

I decided to enroll him at a school in a different area. He began hanging with kids in the neighborhood. He didn't have many friends, but the ones he attracted in that area were into vandalizing properties, committing armed robberies, and any other illicit behavior. This increased my concerns about him attending a neighborhood school.

Shortly after the school year commenced, I received a call from the principal saying that she had video footage of his friends vandalizing a car. Bryshere wasn't in the video, but the principal notified me so that I could keep him away from them. He never had much time to indulge in mischievous activities because I monitored him closely and his curfew dictated he needed to be home 'before the street lights came on.' He would call me at work as soon as he was in the house safely.

Because the kids were punished and my son wasn't, they thought that he told on them. He never did, and I was only contacted because I was an active parent. It didn't matter how much he denied it; they still labeled him as a "snitch." The situation worsened when they initiated fights with him. After the first time, I couldn't believe my eyes when he came home. He had scratches and bruises because of the fights.

Bryshere is a brave person, so he never backed down from anyone. When I finally spoke with the principal in regards to the fights, she said, "There's really nothing I can do other than to talk with the parents and let them know that Bryshere didn't say anything." My son was relentless and begged me to let him fight every day to defend his name. Against my orders, he and one of the kids had a fair fight, but my son beat him up pretty badly. Since he knew he couldn't win, the next time he brought his friends to help him fight.

It escalated to the point where I was afraid for his life. There would be fifteen kids waiting for him after school. I would arrive home after work, and there were threats written on my mail. They were even bold enough to wait for him outside of our home. One day, while Brianna and Bryshere were home alone, my daughter called me frantic saying about twenty kids were waiting for him. She told me they threatened to kick down the door if he didn't come outside. I rushed home! When I finally arrived, about fifty kids were trying to break into my house. I don't even remember shifting the gear into park. I jumped out the car and ran directly to my house to protect my children.

When Bryshere and I had an in-depth discussion about the situation, he let me know when the kids began doing wrong things; he would go in the opposite direction. I couldn't understand their blind rancor because he never got in their way or reported them. By this time, my daughter became exhausted from all of the drama and felt we needed to move. It became an everyday recurrence. I was constantly looking out my front and back doors because we never knew what to expect. When I left in the morning for work, they would come out of the alleyways wearing hoodies, and stand there looking at me. The entire day, I sat at work with all kinds of thoughts and images running through my mind. *Would I come home to see my children badly hurt? Would these kids break into my house and vandalize my property? Would one of them bring a gun and take it further?*

Brianna and Bryshere would get so upset, and both wanted to fight because there were females as part of the mob of kids. I wouldn't let them and was against them fighting. I was tired of calling the cops every day. I couldn't afford to move, and I knew starting over would be impossible. Every decision I made was calculated. I'd dedicated so much time getting Bryshere acclimated to his new school, and getting support from his teachers.

I had enough! I went to the School District of Philadelphia and convinced them to allow my kids to be picked up from my mother's house. This made it better for all of us. The principal had to support my request, and confirm my children were experiencing safety issues. I took off four days without pay just to resolve the issue. That lasted for a while, but then eventually, I called some of my family members because I needed the additional help. It began to feel like David and Goliath - there was always an army of them against the three of us. I was scared for my children's lives. The threats had increased, so I began looking for another school.

To be honest, my son had faced bullying quite a bit through his years in school. As I think back, there were times in grade school where he had issues with being bullied. His class was ridiculously overcrowded. So, I requested that he was assigned to a smaller classroom of

nine students instead of his current cl___
kids. He was teased about it and came
why I had him removed from his p
explained to him that he needed to fo___
distracted by the other kids in his class. I ___ ___ ___that
he wouldn't think that he was the problem. It was a hard
adjustment because he was used to the large classroom
size. I remember him telling me he didn't want to attend
that school anymore.

Most teachers didn't have a full understanding of what
ADHD encompassed. I brought in literature and
educated them. Every child is different, and sometimes, I
had recalcitrant teachers who blatantly said, "I have
another ADHD student in the class, so I already know
what to do." The irony in that statement was; you had to
treat each child accordingly because there had to be a
tailored, individualized plan. No two children are the
same in a traditional classroom, so it's improbable you'll
find the same children with ADHD. I had to educate
myself on how to deal with him on a day to day basis.
What made them think they didn't need to do the same?

Being faced with resistance from some of the faculty
helped me learn to be in control of my emotions. By the
grace of God, I taught myself patience. I had to be more
like an attorney and less like a mother, even though there
were times I couldn't separate the two. I knew once I
approached them in an organized professional manner,
they would have to recognize that I wasn't going to give

so easily. Even more, it confirmed my claims had substance.

For me, coping was about being organized; therefore, I made sure nothing was in disarray. I made folders and put the name of each teacher on it. Inside the folder, was a document which asked for suggestions on how we could improve as a team to help Bryshere become successful while in school. There was an additional document detailing ADHD, its signs, symptoms, and effects of the medication. They were instructed to complete it and bring it to the next meeting. One teacher, in particular, refused to complete it. I contacted the school board and made an appointment to discuss her lack of cooperation. When I arrived at the meeting, I explained the entire situation to them. The school board reacted immediately by contacting the school and forcing the teacher to comply.

Before my kids started going to my mother's house after school, there were times they were home alone from three to eight at night; sometimes until eleven. During that period, Bryshere hung with children in her neighborhood. He began hanging with one boy in particularly. One day I overheard them talking, and didn't like some of what I heard. I didn't agree with his new friend's lifestyle and told my son he couldn't hang with him anymore. Of course, he didn't listen, so I had to walk around the corner to get him from the boy's house later on. When I arrived to get him, the boy began teasing him, as if having a mother who cared was a bad thing. But then I realized that most of those kids lived with their aunts and grandmothers, unlike Bryshere who lived with his mother.

I made sure his hair was always cut, and he was nicely dressed. Most of the guys his age didn't have anyone tending to their needs, so they felt he was a mama's boy. One day after school, I found out he was at the boy's house I previously told him not to hang around. I made him come home immediately because he wasn't supposed to be there. Upon leaving, he took a shortcut through the alleyway and was robbed at gunpoint. Bryshere gave the guy his money, but he also wanted his sneakers. My son refused to give him the sneakers and took off running. The stickup kid pointed the gun and pulled the trigger which jammed. Bryshere escaped with his sneakers and his life.

That was just another incident proving that God had a plan for his life. I would always pray for protection for my children, especially since I wasn't always there. At that point, I knew I had to pray about moving. Even though I couldn't afford it, I knew something had to change. Most of the kids felt resentment toward him because he wasn't permitted to hang with them. I had to be strict because it was becoming increasingly uncomfortable living in a neighborhood that we couldn't enjoy.

The streets wanted my son, and I wasn't letting go. While getting him situated, my daughter started having problems with some girls at school. At the school my children attended, there was a situation with my daughter before my son had his incident. She was around twelve at this time and would have people at the house during the day unbeknownst to me. Bryshere never told on her. Brianna and some of her friends would cut school and have big parties at the house. I had no idea this was happening, but I started paying closer attention because I noticed strange things happening. For example, the groceries would be eaten sooner than I expected. After shopping, the next day everything was just about gone. Even though Bryshere didn't tell on her, she would blame him for the missing food.

I began searching around and found items in the trash can I didn't purchase. There were even condom wrappers in there too. With this discovery, I pretended I was going to work, but didn't. I knew she wouldn't let her friends in through the front door because my neighbors would notice them. Because of that, her only option was to let them in through the back door. I knew if the back door was unlocked, that meant she had let someone inside. As soon as I walked in, I saw more than fifteen kids doing all kinds of things. I didn't bother to ask any questions and started throwing out as many kids as I could. They were so afraid that some of them jumped out of the second-floor window. They even left their coats because they were in such a hurry to leave. That day, I harshly disciplined my daughter.

Bryshere wasn't home when I barged in on the party incident. But when he arrived he saw me disciplining his sister. With the look of confusion on his face, he wanted to know what had happened. Before explaining anything to him, I continued talking to my daughter about everything that occurred. I felt she let her little brother down because he looked to her to be a positive example. It seemed as if she didn't comprehend that I could have lost everything because of the fiasco she arranged. I spoke to both of them and explained how I felt about everything that happened.

Because he was two years younger than her, I couldn't go into depth about the sex and other things I saw. However, he was aware that what she did was disrespectful and unacceptable. They argued about the situation, and he teased her about getting punished. He shed light on the fact that he always tried to tell me that he wasn't the one eating all the food. He said Brianna blamed him, knowing it was her friends all along. After he had told me that, I apologized to him, and we hugged. I felt sorry for not listening to him. Since he ate all the food due in the past due to the side effects of his medicine, I didn't believe him. Surprisingly, during our discussion, Brianna was very disrespectful. I let them know when you misbehave, you have to pay the consequences, so I sent her to stay with my mother for three months.

Bryshere enjoyed having me to himself while she stayed with my mother. He was excited to spend more time with me. During that time, we went to therapy together and tried working through our issues. I had him discuss how he felt about not having her at the house. I made his schedule and put it on his door so that he could be more independent. I was still working two jobs so I couldn't spend as much time with him as I wanted. With Brianna not being there, he had extra chores. Since he had more responsibilities, I started teaching him how to maintain the house by himself.

When she finally returned, we had to rebuild our bond. She was upset with me and felt that I favored Bryshere. That wasn't true at all. I didn't want to send her away, and I hadn't stopped loving her. The time away was for her to reflect on her malapropos behavior. The behavioral issues with my children were happening at once, and it weighed on me heavily. Even though her actions were wrong, she didn't grasp the severity of what she had done. Her punishment was perceived as me not wanting her anymore. I was more disappointed than angry. As the months passed, I knew I needed her back at home. For that reason, I didn't allow it to exceed more than three months. We needed to resolve this as a family, and we couldn't do that with her living somewhere else.

She was already experiencing emotional frustrations because I wasn't with her father, so this was added stress.

When she and I attended therapy, we addressed her feelings. Her thoughts were since I sent her to my mother's house, which indicated I was more than upset. During our session, she spoke about how it was hard not having a male figure at home. She also mentioned my hectic work schedule, which was a recurring issue. I think as a parent, I did the best that I could with the knowledge I had. Even if there was a parenting manual available, to prepare you for specific issues; each child is different. Because of that, you don't know what circumstances will arise at any given time. Since I was so young when they were born, I was maturing while raising my children. Ironically, it was like we were raised together. I had to figure out the proper way to parent on my own. Nonetheless, at this point, I couldn't make excuses. I needed a better solution to our problems, and I needed it quickly.

***

Part of my growth and maturing was learning how to ask for help when there was something that I didn't know. Sometimes, I would take some of the things that Bryshere did personally. I had to learn not to do that in any situation. At times, when he was disciplined, he would punch the wall. I became frustrated and took it as a form of disrespectful. Once, I evaluated my reactions; I learned that having a discussion with him was much more efficient. I asked, "Why were you angry? Why did you punch the wall?" His reasoning was he couldn't remember the multiple tasks I had assigned him to do, so he became frustrated. He thought he would get punished if he didn't complete all of them, so he became angry and felt compelled to hit the wall. As a single parent, sometimes it happened that way. When I arrived home, I was tired, so I instructed him in several directions. It wasn't his fault. Because of that, I learned how to give him individual tasks and wait for him to finish them one at a time.

I was also dealing with the frustration of his behavior at school. It didn't matter what school he attended; there were issues. Even if other children partook in the bad behavior, he didn't know when to stop. Due to his behavior, he was assigned a 504, which is a plan developed to ensure that a child who has a disability identified under the law and is attending an elementary or secondary educational institution receives accommodations that will ensure their academic success and access to the learning environment. According to his plan between the school and parents, there were set goals so that he wouldn't be held responsible for things that were a manifestation of his disorder. We received an initial packet from the state of Pennsylvania that outlined the bylaws and regulations. He was also assigned an advocate, which are individuals who speak out on the best interests of children. They typically seek to protect children's rights which may be abridged or abused in a number of areas. I was educated about our rights and all the things that were allotted to my child. The packet even included sample letters to copy if you needed to draft a letter to arrange an IEP hearing.

I called the advocate, and she educated me on everything I needed to know. From the operations of the IEP program to knowing how to write an appeal, I absorbed all of the information that she provided. In his IEP plan, it stated that he had an additional thirty minutes to take an exam. Because he couldn't sit idle for more than thirty minutes at a time, he was allowed the extra time. I developed a relationship with his homeroom teacher who gathered information from the other teachers detailing his performance in his classes. He emailed all correspondence, or he called me when Bryshere's behavior needed to be redirected. Sometimes, he put my son on the phone so that his behavior was addressed immediately. This proved to be very helpful and productive. Any issue I needed to be aware of was handled and never lingered. If there were violations, such as him receiving too many detentions; we would have to reevaluate to see if it was a manifestation of his disorder. If this were the case, I would contest the decision to punish him excessively.

At times, I wasn't pleased with the way the school dealt with his behavior, so I had lawyers advocate for Bryshere and educate me on the way to fight for his rights. Their services were pro bono, which helped financially. It was mandatory for Bryshere to be present and participate in most of the meetings. Certain aspects of information couldn't be discussed in front of him, so he wasn't required to be there during those times. I made it clear that he was prohibited to use his disorder as a cause to misbehave. I instilled in him that he wasn't defined by his condition. I told him to pray and ask God to help him cope with his issues.

I understood that he only wanted to be a typical kid; to me, he was. He didn't see it that way, even though nothing about the way I treat him would suggest otherwise. I did my best to make sure he had an everyday teenage life. Even his sister treated him as a typical little brother. I didn't have to tell her to treat him that way; she did it innately. If he went into her room without asking, she reacted the same way she would have before he was diagnosed.

I recall certain incidents when he hid the phone so that she couldn't talk to her friends. That ignited arguments between them because she loved being on the phone. His reasoning was he wanted to use the phone as well. I had to implement a plan where they each received a degree of time on the phone. Those were the two issues they bickered about most – being in her room without permission and hiding the phone. There was another problem that arose often. Whenever she left to visit her father, there was tension in the house. Bryshere didn't have his father to visit, so this disconcerted him. Even though her father wasn't always there, they had a relationship, and she visited him on the weekends. She voiced the activity filled weekend she anticipated, and it bothered my son tremendously. When she spoke about it, it wasn't in a bragging or teasing manner. She was merely elated and couldn't contain her excitement. I didn't want him to feel left out, so I had my father spend time with him on the weekends sometimes. I always made sure that when Bryshere wasn't with me, my parents were able to handle him. He had a relationship with his father's side, but it was much different. To this day, my daughter says that I coddled him too much. My reason for keeping him tightly by my side was simple; leaving him in the care of other people would require him to be disciplined. I didn't want anyone to hurt him and refused to let that happen.

As he started to become more social, it was important that I knew all of his friends. Whenever I learned he was hanging with someone; I became a private investigator. I made sure I obtained as much information as I could about the people he wanted to befriend. It was my priority to check on him, and I made it my business to be informed of every detail. I had to meet the mother, father, or guardian as well as visit their home. Even though I still had reservations after my visits, I needed to observe the lifestyle of his friend and their family. I soon realized that no matter the extent of my thoroughness, he and I still had disagreements if the parents of his associates weren't dedicated to their children.

The bullying situations were some of the most trying times I experienced. It was so intense when he transferred schools; the principal permitted him to get there early just to avoid the children trying to fight him. She allowed him to come to school early and leave early. He would then go to my neighbor's house until I ended my work day. The entire time at work, I was nervous and terrified. All I thought about was the aftermath of him walking outside or going to the store. Bryshere was fearless and didn't listen; I always feared those kids would attack him if he were alone.

I had so many things in place to keep him safe. There was a police officer that followed him home and then called me when he was in the house safely. Then, when my daughter arrived home, she called me and let me know everything was okay. I, in turn, called and checked on them every hour. At that point, I developed severe anxiety and notified my boss. I apologized in advance, anticipating the need to leave work abruptly. They hunted him like he was prey every day so I couldn't let down my guard for a second. I cried so much during that time because I was so afraid they were going to kill my son. The police couldn't arrest any of the kids because they hadn't committed the assault. It was rough. Imagine trying to keep your child away from the streets, but the streets kept trying to pull him in.

This continued for approximately a year. Eventually, the kids were tired of trying to get to him to avail. Some of them were arrested for other situations, and some moved to other neighborhoods. One day, it just all settled down. It was like God had answered my prayers!

By now, his grades had dwindled. I thought it was because the school didn't have the proper resources to help him, but it was because of the bullying. I knew that I couldn't keep Bryshere from hanging out with everyone. I noticed that as he became older, he made wiser decisions about his friends. He had one particular friend who went to the studio with him. Sometimes they would be with his older brother who was an aspiring rapper. I didn't think he was involved with the streets, but I had my concerns. I wasn't sure if he was jealous or envious about all the attention Bryshere was receiving. They had their disagreements probably because of the competitiveness, so they went their separate ways.

He had another friend he met through a summer program at church. We called him Buck, and he was also the child of a single mother. He was a prankster and enjoyed Bryshere's company. He supported my son at his games and all of his other endeavors. He was a much closer friend to Bryshere than any other person. Buck was always very genuine, and had a lot of respect for the family; he became a part of our family. I don't think any of his friends knew about his ADHD, but I think Buck had an inkling that there was something beneath it all that we didn't necessarily mention. I vividly remember while they were playing a video game, I asked Bryshere why he didn't wash the dishes. It was like Buck picked up on his energy and said, "Let's just do the dishes so that mom won't be mad. Then, we can clean up your room." It was like he knew to guide Bryshere, even though he may not have known the underlying reason. Buck was one of his truest friends. The last time we saw him was at my birthday party about a year ago. They hadn't seen each other in a while, but just like brothers, they picked up right where they last ended.

PART TWO

YAZZ THE GREATEST

CHAPTER SEVEN

There's rampant poverty, drug addiction, senseless murders and fatherless homes filled with single mothers throughout our city. I was overprotective of my son because he was a young black male and didn't have his father in his life. I think back to when I took him to sports practice. I noticed how men treated me differently because I was a woman raising him alone. One of the coaches said, "He can play in a starting position if you let me take you to dinner." I always declined. Bryshere disliked the negative attention I received and tried to keep me from waiting there. I drove him to practice, so the harassment was unavoidable.

He was already going through a lot because of his ADHD. There were things that I didn't allow either of my children to do and people I kept people away from them. I was considered a strict parent. Knowing that's how I was depicted made me more protective because that meant I was doing something right. If I asked them to do something, and it wasn't done when I arrived home; I woke them from their sleep. I didn't care if it was midnight. They had clear instructions and chose to disregard them, so I made them do it at that very moment.

At school, whenever they accused him of doing something wrong, I investigated it fully. If I hadn't, he would've been mandated to a school like the Community Education Partners. CEP, as it's called in Philadelphia, was a disciplinary school injected into the school system. It primarily used computer-based instruction to minimize the chance for student interaction. The typical student who entered a CEP school failed three or more subjects, was suspended three or more times and had a poor attendance record at their school. Not only did my son not fall into any of those categories; there wasn't any support to help him with his condition. I battled with the schools constantly so that he wouldn't become a statistic. Even when they did accept his disorder, they refused to incorporate certain things into their classrooms. I visited his school almost twice a week. I always called and emailed the teachers to keep an open line of communication. I asked to be notified about his grades in advance. When I asked about his progress, they always said he was doing fine. For me, being proactive was better than waiting until he received his report card.

Whenever they failed to inform me about the subjects he struggled with; I made sure he was given the extended thirty days to complete his work. The debacle was a direct result of their lack of communication. It was unfair that I wasn't able to address the issues beforehand and he had the right to deal with those areas. If I didn't know about his particular rights, the school would have never allowed him to make up his work. They assigned him an extensive amount of makeup work, but we indeed completed it all.

I was successful in helping him make up his assignments, and he increased his grades. I was unable to work overtime because he needed help with his work. I knew the bills were being neglected, but I had to make a choice for my son.

One of Bryshere's strengths was that he dedicated himself to things of interest. In the beginning, I thought he was going to be a football player because of his commitment to the sport. Then, as he showed passion in other things, I knew that he was going to be a celebrity at some point in his life. I didn't know what industry; I just knew it was going to happen. So, I made sure he remained involved in the activities that he loved.

By fourteen, he was a star football player at Overbrook, but he sustained two major injuries during a game. As the running back, he was supposed to run a touchdown play that was arranged for him. Instead, the quarterback ran a play that they didn't discuss, and the ball flew over his head. He fumbled the ball but recovered it so that the other team wouldn't get it. As he attempted to get up, the biggest player on the other team jumped on top of him, and his arm snapped in two places. Even with his arm dangling from the injury, Bryshere held the ball with his other hand, ran ten yards and scored the touchdown. He didn't realize he was hurt until he scored the touchdown; then he collapsed. The injuries were so severe he was stabilized on the field and placed on the stretcher. He even had a concussion. They took him to the area hospital, and in the emergency room, they manually shifted his arm back into place. Even though they numbed the area, he still felt the pain. He belted a loud scream that was the worse sound that I'd ever heard. They put a cast on it because they couldn't operate until the swelling went down. When he finally had surgery, he was in the hospital for two days and had three months of recovery. After that eye-opening experience, I made up my mind about his future as a football player and prayed that he felt the same way.

While he was recovering from his injuries, he began rapping. At first, I wasn't aware of it because he did it behind my back. I didn't have a disdain for rap music; I had an issue with the excessive profanity and vulgar content. When he and his sister volunteered at my job, he met a producer named Gates. He was like a brother to me, so he and Bryshere became friends. He visited his studio regularly for almost a year before I knew about it.

One evening, Gates called and told me that my son was rapping on some tracks they recorded together. He insisted I listen to his music. Before I could get upset, he played a song. Once I heard it, I said, "Effective immediately; I am now Bryshere's manager!"

Gates replied, "Okay good, but his name isn't Bryshere, it's 'Yazz the Greatest.'"

I immediately repeated, "'Yazz the Greatest?' Okay, I'm Yazz's manager!" My son sounded that good. Gates and I agreed to manage him together and 'Yazz the Greatest' was born. Right then, I made a choice to no longer call my son by his given name; I call him Yazz.

Interestingly enough my foray into the world of entertainment as a manager began while I was working at the hospital. It was there that I became close with a young lady who would eventually come to ask me to manage her daughter's rap group, Kimo. She felt that I had what it took to help the group garner attention and push their career further. Besides, she also liked my personality. With the exception of being fourteen years old, the group had a sound similar to that of legendary female rap group, Salt-N-Pepa. My priority as their new manager was to begin booking sessions in various studios across Philadelphia. It wasn't long before a few of the elite acts of the city's music scene, such as Musiq Soulchild, Kindred the Family Soul and The Roots took notice of the girls and began to feature them on a few of their songs. Soon after, the girls began to perform at The Black Lily, an open mic established by The Roots.

To take full advantage of the momentum that Kimo was beginning to build, I started to frequent clubs and events to position myself to meet industry insiders and others who were able to play a role in advancing their career. My plan worked, and pretty soon the girls were being interviewed by the Daily News. With their parent's permission and approval, I booked them for club performances. More people began to take notice, and compliments on their maturity and talent poured in. The club dates were a hit, and before long Kimo was on tour with The Roots performing at various House of Blues across the nation. The joy and passion I felt knowing that I played an integral part in making the dreams of Kimo come true, confirmed that I was called to be a manager.

Over the next seven years, I continued to manage them. During this time their popularity grew, and they attracted the attention of the likes of Philadelphia rapper, Eve. Although she was unable to work with Kimo due to her busy schedule, she was gracious enough to reach out to Timbaland who felt there was a chance that the girls could get a recording deal with Missy Elliot and Violator Records. The deal never came to fruition. Unbeknownst to me, there was a third party involved with Kimo who needed to be included in all negotiations for them to be able to move forward. As time passed, negotiations stalled. It was all well and good, as by this time the girls were older and had slowly grown apart. It wasn't long before Kimo eventually broke up and I decided to take a break from managing and the entertainment industry.

***

While I was segueing away from the entertainment industry, my son was harboring a secret desire to enter the world from which I was exiting. I knew at the beginning of his career; he would have a lot of pressure on him. So, I had to figure out who he was as an artist. I encouraged him to be himself and let him know it was okay to be different. He didn't have to be like anyone else, especially in entertainment. I would soon learn that God's plan for my son's career wasn't about my management skills; it was about what He had already ordained.

Before I began to help Yazz with his career, he was paying for everything on his own. To cover his expenses, he had the foresight to get a job at Pizza Hut, as their mascot. It was his responsibility to hand out coupons and entice people to come inside the restaurant. When he told me he worked at Pizza Hut, I just assumed that he worked as a cook, until I had to pick him up from work one day. When I pulled into the parking lot, I noticed the mascot was dancing and fun. It brought a smile to face, and that's when I realized it was him. My son was the mascot. He eventually convinced the manager that although he was great at being the mascot, his skills would be better served to work as a cook; and the manager agreed. Unfortunately, he was just too greedy and got fired because he couldn't stop eating the chicken.

Although his job at Pizza Hut was short-lived, I was proud of him for going out and getting a job, particularly because he did it on his volition. I admired that he was a dedicated and hard worker that didn't use his disorder or make excuses when it was time to get things done. Yazz was a go-getter. He wasn't just going to sit back and rely on his mother to handle everything for him. He wasn't a lazy child by any stretch of the imagination and had absolutely no qualms about starting at the bottom and working his way up to the top. He always gave one hundred percent to anything he did and didn't need anyone to coddle him. He was able to go in, listen to what he needed to do and get it done. I think seeing these qualities in him at such a young age is what inspired to help him reach his dream of being a rapper.

***

After seeing that Yazz had secured a job to finance his career, I started arranging everything. All his studio time went through me, and they made sure that I approved everything. At this point, I realized there were thousands of rappers in the city. I needed maximum exposure and had to set him apart from the rest. I didn't want him being a gangster rapper and making music filled with foul language. If he had to use an inappropriate word or two, he asked me to leave the studio out of respect.

He started performing at local bars and open mic contests. We met other up-and-coming Philadelphia rap artists, like 'Lee Mazin' and 'Young Savage.' At this time, they would all hang out together. Often, I drove Young Savage home because I didn't want him catching the bus so late. They were all still young and had school the next day.

We supported Young Savage so much; people thought that he and Yazz were a local rap group. His manager wanted my son to be the hype man for Young Savage, but I didn't allow it because Yazz was an artist and had the talent. The manager and I had a heated discussion about the hype man situation. Since I wouldn't give my consent, he didn't allow him to perform his songs during Young Savage's shows.

Eventually, I told Yazz that he needed to separate himself and focus on his brand. I wanted him to do something different, so I decided to find some backup dancers. My background was in dance, so I knew what to look for in performers. We held an audition, and hired ten female dancers I later named 'The Yazzettes.' I had the girls and their parents sign contracts. I enforced a no tolerance policy because he was a young man and they were young girls. I made sure there was proper conduct and positive representation at all times. No drugs, no drinking or dating the artists was permitted. We practiced three hours a day, three days a week and prayed together before our shows.

When Yazz was fifteen, he and Tyriq Lamont, a hometown comedian, filmed a short film, which would later be uploaded to YouTube, in my home. I was blown away by my son's talent and acting skills. He was at ease in front of the camera and had a natural charisma obvious to anyone who saw the short film. It was immediately obvious to me as well. I know mothers are typically biased when it comes to their children, but his talent was undeniable. The short film received over one million views on YouTube. With the newfound knowledge of his acting ability, I realized that Yazz had the capacity to be an all-around entertainer and encouraged him to consider other avenues of the arts. Although his first love was rapping, it was a very real possibility that his blessings could come from somewhere else in the entertainment world and I told him as such.

Although his natural acting ability was unquestionable, I was keenly aware that acting classes would only stand to improve upon skills. The issue was, I just couldn't afford to enroll Yazz in any of them. My suggested solution was for him to search online and to study the techniques found in videos and outlined in articles. Along with his dedication, the sight of my son honing his skills awakened a feeling in me that he was going to take the world by storm. With his best interest in mind, I continued ahead in manager mode.

While Yazz's focus on acting was underway, in his heart, he was a rapper and performer first. I scheduled more rehearsal times and coordinated dancers for future shows. I was impressed when Yazz expressed that he wanted to learn how to dance to add dimension to his performances. So, of course, I put someone in place that could work with him and teach what he needed to know. I was sure to keep his asthma in mind when scheduling his practices so as not bring about any attacks. The more he prepared, the more hectic both of our weeks became. Between his rehearsals and shows, we spent a lot of time on the road. It came to the point that I had to schedule my duties at the hospital around my work with him. It was well worth it, and I would have done it a thousand times over. He was my son, and I would do whatever it took to help him see his dreams come true. There were many times I willingly sacrificed my income tax return to ensure the look of his performance and team were just right.

As an artist, I always treated him like he was a celebrity. We had security with us at all times because females were all over him and guys would be jealous sometimes. At one of his performances at a smaller venue, I only took three backup dancers. The show was about to begin, and we couldn't locate Yazz. I didn't want to start the show without him present, but I reluctantly started it anyway hoping he would appear on stage. As soon as the lights came on, he did a surprise introduction. He had on a mask and slid down the banister with one of his dancers! That's when I really saw his star potential. Black Thought, a member of The Roots, told me on many occasions that Yazz was going to be a star. He believed in him so much that he became his mentor.

After a while, I felt like I was being undervalued. I would make excuses during rehearsals when things didn't go smoothly, which was often. I decided not to participate with the arranging of his upcoming show or be a part of the team any longer. He continued preparing for the show and then invited me to attend. I still supported him, so of course, I went to the rehearsal.

When I arrived, the show was in such disarray I changed it completely. Lauriel, one of the lead dancers, expressed her feelings of joy, and so did the other dancers. In my absence, Lauriel's mother stepped in and made sure Yazz was okay. She also helped take care of the other girls.

In rehearsals what stood out the most, was that they had a chance to be kids. They had fun and danced in competitions against each other. They were all talented, so they showcased their abilities to prove who was the best. It was bittersweet because dancers would get older, move on to other things or matriculate into college. This meant, we had to audition more dancers. Auditions were often held. When the new girls became part of the team, some of the veteran dancers didn't like Yazz directing his attention toward them. Some of the dancers were even upset with me because I paid close attention to Lauriel. It's not that I favored her, I just knew she had an extensive dance resume. I asked her to help choreograph and teach the routines because dance was her life. While the other dancers had other things that occupied their time; she was always practicing and honing her craft.

I was so proud of how Yazz handled himself when it came to the different aspects of his career. He wasn't just a rap artist. He took the time to learn the choreography so that he could teach it to his dancers. He was very active in every aspect of his performances and shows. Many of the dancers were inspired by that. During rehearsals, Yazz was strict and so was I. He had a live band, so he taught them how to listen to the music and dance to the rhythm. Unlike a recorded track, the sounds are different when a band plays a song. Because he understood that, he took the time to make sure they were in sync with the music. I believe that's why things went so well for his brand. We all worked without ever being paid. For them to remain part of the team showed how much they respected and believed in him.

As my son's popularity began to grow, so did my responsibility to his career and in no time I was wearing various hats. I was his manager, band manager, road manager, transportation, and mother. I put together a promotional team to represent his brand. Everyone on his team, including security, looked professional and cohesive wearing the black 'Team Yazz' t-shirts that I provided. I hustled to get whatever it was my son needed to make sure that he and his team, had everything for his performance to be perfect. On some occasions, this meant using my entire tax refund to make the necessary purchases. On others, it meant scurrying to Forman Mills, a discount retail chain, to buy t-shirts, then taking them to a different county to get them printed and returning to pick them up just before Yazz's show. There were times that I arrived at a show, and I had to fight with team members who wanted to wear their clothes instead of the 'Team Yazz' shirts. In so many words I let them know that wasn't an option. They were 'Team Yazz' when they were with us, no questions, and their outfits would represent as such.

One night, they performed at a show called 'Don't Shoot' at Temple University. Yazz was performing, and about twenty of our team members were standing in the back wearing 'Team Yazz' shirts. I had a shirt made for everyone, but one of the male dancers refused to wear it. When my son found out, they began fighting backstage. I was furious that he stepped outside of his professionalism. After seeing the fight, Lauriel's mother became skeptical about having her continue with the team. I had to calm her down. She was the youngest dancer, and her mother knew that I wouldn't intentionally put her in any danger.

After that unfortunate situation, I made sure it was understood that I handled all things. Especially issues that would cause him to become upset. Everybody wouldn't understand that he was dealing with a disorder, so it was best that I resolved any disagreements. Only the male dancer knew that he had ADHD because they were good friends. I expressed the ways to handle Yazz to avoid future situations. This helped, and it allowed him not to take things personally. I let my son know that he needed to express himself without reverting to his past behavior. He still hadn't reached the point where he could walk away from a heated moment. I didn't want that to ruin what he enjoyed doing, especially because I saw the potential he had. I witnessed his dedication and effort, so

I didn't want it to all be in vain. Thankfully, once Yazz understood what was at stake, he approached his career differently than he did school. Music was something he didn't have to struggle to understand, and he was finally speaking his language.

***

Despite our occasional ups and down, Yazz had a very close knit team. Nevertheless, only a select few members of the team knew about his ADHD. If ever there was an incident stemming from the disorder I would cover for him. The incidents were few and far between because if I sensed an issue arising, I would let him step away to get the break that he needed. Even so, the bond between all of us was tight. We had each other's backs, and we knew how each other worked, including knowing when we needed to step in for one another. With Yazz having asthma and him putting his full energy into his performances, there were times when he needed to catch his breath for a few moments. His DJ could sense this and would spin the tracks in a unique way giving Yazz the time he needed.

Dealing with Yazz's team was easy compared to the other challenges I faced. Many of my issues stemmed from my appearance. First of all, I was obviously a woman in a male-dominated industry. Second of all, I appeared to be younger than my actual age. These two superficial factors played largely into how I was treated and how my requests were met, or in some cases not met.

I had to fight for simple standards like sound checks for Yazz and spot checks for his dancers. Their responses were always the same: he didn't need a soundcheck because he was a rapper. Likewise, my reply never changed: "Yes he does." The people I went up against failed to realize that regardless of how they chose to handle Yazz's shows, I was going to fight tooth and nail to make certain that he had what he needed for a top-notch performance. The way I saw it, they had two choices; adhere to the standard and meet my requests or attempt to pull a power move and in the end, still meet my requests.

I experienced blatant sexism on many occasions. The perception that I would be willing to use sex to advance Yazz's career loomed over many of my interactions with men in the industry. Because of how I was raised, I treated everyone kindly; however, it was not always received as I had intended. Where I saw courtesy and caring, they saw an opportunity. I drew a line in the sand early on, and anyone who dared to cross it learned quickly they were better off where they stood. I wasn't that type of person, and better still, I wasn't that kind of mother. Everything I was doing was for Yazz, and there was no way that I would do anything to jeopardize his career or his opinion of me.

I remember one such occasion when a man thought that my body was fair game because of what he may have been able to do for Yazz. Initially, I contacted him with the hopes that he would be able to assist me with a project that I had in mind. As one would expect, he arranged a meeting to discuss my idea. When I walked into the room with my son, the look of shock was splayed across his face. He apparently expected that it would be only us at the meeting.

At the conclusion of our discussion, I stood to leave, and the man, as if it were his right, touched my behind. In that one brief moment, he had flagrantly disregarded the boundaries of personal space and disrespected my son and me. I didn't present myself as anything other than a manager working in the best interest of her client. Yet, he still perceived me as a woman only good enough to provide a sexual favor. I was angry, hurt and uncomfortable, but mostly I was grateful that Yazz didn't see the disrespect. He was fiercely protective of me, and I would never want him to feel as if he could not defend me.

Needless to say, we never worked with the man after he realized I was not his plaything, and that his advances were reviled. Years later, we came in contact with him again when one of his clients and Yazz had a show together at the TLA, which is the Theater of Living Arts located on South Street. By that time, the man and I didn't have any problems because I had set the tone that demanded my son and me to be respected.

Nothing was worth doing something that I would've regretted. I made it my point to maintain my dignity and my worth. Being a woman in the industry was difficult enough without me running the risk of damaging either of our reputations; especially before we had fully established ourselves. Appearance and false expectations aside, I knew how to intelligently and efficiently get my point across without being loud or disrespectful. And I knew that it would be my son's talent that took him to the next level, not my body.

There weren't many people who believed in the vision he had for himself and my support of that vision. However, I had a select few male friends that consistently came to support his performances. I remember a promoter of a show at the TLA, attempted to interrupt his performance while he was still on stage. It was infuriating because he wasn't cutting anyone else's show, but because my son was an up and coming artist, he was trying to treat him differently. A male friend of mine, who happened to be at the show, came to his defense and demanded that he be able to finish his full set. Thankfully, the matter was rectified, and he was able to complete his set.

In addition to battling chauvinistic attitudes, I faced financial challenges. To put it bluntly, I didn't have enough money. Just as I had found a creative solution for Yazz's acting classes, I discovered low cost or free methods to develop him as an artist. I established partnerships with people who not only believed in my son, but also had an interest in cultivating his career. I was grateful to have found so many people who knew that I couldn't afford to pay them and were still willing to work for free simply because they believed in him. I had an entire team from promotions to security, and they were all working for free. It was beautiful, and I was sincerely appreciative for all of their help.

The Heat Factory Studio, located in the Southwest section of Philadelphia, and Batcave Studio, located in the North section of Philadelphia, were two partners that lent a great deal of support to Yazz in music, as well as in life. Ruggy the engineer, who is also one of the owners of Batcave Studio, appreciated my vision for Yazz's education, career and used studio time to motivate him academically. If he misbehaved in school or fell below my expectations in class, Ruggy would not allow him to be in the studio. For this and much more, I sincerely appreciated him. Yazz's sessions often ran from about four-thirty in the afternoon to eleven o'clock in the evening, and during these times Ruggy never forgot that he was a student. From time to time he would let Yazz use his office to complete his assignments. His partner would even go so far as to help Yazz with his homework.

In fact, it was at the Batcave that my son would forever become 'Yazz' to Ruggy. Upon initially meeting Ruggy, the first thing he asked my son was why he called himself 'Yazz The Greatest.' With the utmost confidence, he replied that he derived 'Yazz' from the internet; however 'The Greatest' was him speaking his greatness into existence. Ruggy was impressed to hear a teenager speak in such a manner, as was I.

***

The Batcave was like a second home to Yazz, and he stayed there with Ruggy for about two years. There he found comfort and the opportunity to surround himself with others who shared his love of music. Although he had a personality that people were naturally drawn to, he wasn't as social as one would expect of someone his age. Frankly, it was for no other reason that the fact that his thoughts revolved around music. Local artists who also recorded at the Batcave began to develop respect for Yazz as he began to showcase his skills. People weren't expecting him to be as talented as he was and were often surprised. When they would hear him rap, they would compliment how different he was and encouraged him to stay true to his style. From live-streaming his sessions to providing tips to enhance his flow, artists that supported him were always there to lend a helping hand if ever it was needed.

Because I raised Yazz to stay positive and to be mindful of how he carried himself, he was conscious of his interactions with other artists. He didn't have any beef with other artists because I discouraged it and on the off chance I felt like there was something brewing I would do my best to diffuse it immediately. I wanted to see young black men sticking together, especially in Philadelphia.

One such demonstration of support came from none other than Philadelphia rap legend, Beanie Sigel. Yazz was at the Batcave filming a video when Ruggy expressed that he thought something was missing. Being who I am, and knowing that the Hip-Hop great was in the studio at that very moment, I took it upon myself to ask Beans to do a cameo for Yazz's video. He agreed, came over and did an introduction in the video for the song, *Need a Bad Chick*.

Artists who were familiar with my relationship with Yazz would share their stories and how they wished they had mothers who supported them and their careers. Some even began to look at me as a motherly figure and started calling me Mom. Before speaking to them, I don't think Yazz saw what I was doing as atypical or outside of my responsibilities as a mother. It's my belief that these conversations put my confidence in and support of his talent and career into perspective. He began to understand that I was doing what I did because I wanted to, not because I had to. But in all honesty, whether he understood it or not; regardless if he chose to recognize it or not, my actions would have remained the same. That's how strong my faith in him was and still is.

Though the love from others was there, not everyone thought that I was the best person to manage my son's career. Although Yazz would come to my defense, some outsiders felt that having a mother for a manager would spell disaster. They thought that it was a conflict of interest and we would constantly argue. My response was, they didn't know me, nor did they know there was no conflict of interest because everything I did was for Yazz, not me. I always warned him that if someone was rallying to keep away the one person whose sole interest was in his favor, then they were probably doing something they shouldn't be doing.

I remember clearly this one occasion when a gentleman was interested in Yazz being a part of his crew. Logically speaking, I felt it was safe to assume that it was because he saw in him what everyone else saw; a star. However to my surprise, when it came time to discuss the particulars of Yazz joining the crew, the gentleman turned out to be condescending and ill-mannered. Instead of selling to me why my son would make a great addition to his crew, he chose to allude that Yazz needed the crew because he was incapable of making it on his own. The gentleman all but said my son was 'a nobody.' As it can be imagined, the rest of the conversation did not go well. Naturally, the gentleman fell out of my favor. I don't recall the explanation that I gave to Yazz as to why the becoming part of the crew didn't work out, but I never shared with him what the gentleman said. It would have only served to discourage him. However, the effect on me was just the opposite. It added fuel to my flame and inspired me to go harder for my son.

The most personal challenges that I faced as Yazz's manager was the separation of our familial and business relationships. Of course, I was his mother first and foremost, so he never failed to give me my due respect. However, the dynamic of our relationship changed and it became harder for me not to blur the lines. Almost overnight I went from enforcing his nightly curfew to being his employee. The reality of my situation was that he was the artist and I was the manager. I was a part of his team and worked for his brand. He was my boss.

There would be exchanges and intense arguments between us that weren't typical of a mother and son. I had to make a conscious effort to speak to him differently and to respect that he was no longer a child, but a young man who was making his own money. Around this time, Yazz was getting booked to perform at Sweet Sixteen birthday parties and other celebratory events, where he was demanding between $1,200 and $2,000 for a one-hour performance. And he was well worth the rate.

In addition to putting on a great show, Yazz would bring flowers and gift cards for the young ladies and gift cards to the young men who had hired him. He, under no obligation and without a trace of annoyance or air of arrogance, took pictures and signed autographs for the guests of honor and their invitees. Parents would be so impressed with his professionalism and manners that they would refer him to others who were planning parties. As his manager I was pleased; however, as his mother, I was unabashedly proud of his behavior. He was, in fact professional, but it was more than that. How he handled himself, and the little things he did to go the extra mile were a part of who he was. It was nothing he learned; it was from inside. He was thoughtful and self-assured, but remained gracious, never arrogant.

Every performance did not start out as smoothly as those at the private parties, yet Yazz was always able to read the crowd's energy as soon as he stepped on stage. He would then either cater to it or sway it in a positive direction. He would throw his all into a performance and pretty soon the crowd would get excited. So, by the end of each performance, crowds who may not have been the most receptive early on became instant fans. They always had something positive to say about the show. Yazz wasn't easily discouraged when it came to his music. He always went hard and remained steadfast. These attributes, along with his attention to detail, is a part of what makes him a great entertainer.

I learned quickly that the world of entertainment isn't just about talent. And regardless of how hard you try to do your job and be a good person; there is always someone or something lurking trying to bring you harm. Just before Yazz was due to hit the stage for a performance at the TLA. I received a text message that read: *When you're son comes outside, we're going to kill him.* The words blurred in front of me as I began to tremble. My heart beat rapidly as I surveyed his dancers and security for information on possible issues or altercations with anyone; there were none.

My only recourse, or so I thought, was to cancel the autograph and picture session scheduled at the end of his performance. Yazz didn't agree with me and immediately replied, "No," to my suggestion. He felt in spite of what was going on around us; his supporters still deserved all they expected from him. My thoughts raced through all those who could have sent the text and settled on a young lady who I had asked to stop coming around. Afterward, she started messaging me on Facebook, sending disrespectful messages and subliminal posts on Instagram, so I had a feeling that this latest text message was from her.

By the time the show had finished, and Yazz met with his supporters, I reached the conclusion that it was not safe for him to simply go home as if I had never received the text message. I thought it was better to err on the side of caution. I had armed security escort him to a hotel, where I felt he would be safe. I stayed at my mother's that night. I can still remember the way I felt when I got the text. It's not a feeling that a mother should ever have to experience.

Thankfully, the text message was the only occurrence of such threats in his professional career. I thank God daily for that because hatred and jealousy often accompany the pursuit of your dreams in any industry. Moreover, dreams are powerful beyond measure, and the strength they gave Yazz was immeasurable. I didn't ever want to be the person to take any of that away from him because I feared for his well-being. He deserved everything that awaited him, and I am eternally grateful that no one has ever again tried to take it away from with threats or intimidation.

Yazz's strength often made me realize how important it is to trust in God. Whenever I wanted to back down or if I was unsure of a situation, he would say 'no.' Not in a careless way, but in a way that let me know that he had trust that God would protect him no matter what.

***

As my son continued to put on great performances, word spread about 'Yazz The Greatest' and Philadelphia personalities and events, took notice and showed love. When he was just seventeen, Yazz was booked to perform at the nation's largest African-American street festival, the Odunde Festival in Philadelphia where Hip-Hop pioneer, Big Daddy Kane was the headliner. When Yazz's set wrapped, Big Daddy Kane acknowledged his performance and talked to him for about fifteen minutes, giving him words of wisdom. Those fifteen minutes were golden.

I hadn't heard from my ex-fiancé in a while, until my son started making a name for himself and was already recognized as a rapper throughout Philadelphia. When Yazz needed an older male to talk to, my ex-fiancé wasn't there. One day, he called me and asked if my son could do an interview with a very popular local online magazine. The magazine contacted him because they didn't have my information. I agreed to the interview with the stipulation of them conducting it in the studio where my son was recording. My ex-fiancé noticed the hard work Yazz and I were putting into his project, and was very proud of us.

He started telling people he was the father of my son. When people asked my son if my ex-fiancé was his father, Yazz let them know we were previously engaged and he considered him his stepfather while we were engaged. My son knew it meant a lot for my ex-fiancé to be acknowledged in public. Even though he was not in his life full-time, we felt it wasn't necessary to reveal that to other people. After a while, I continually rejected his propositions of pursuing a relationship again. He couldn't separate our friendship from our previous romance. Eventually, it became a toxic friendship.

On several occasions, I made it very clear we would never get back together. I always made an effort to keep my business and personal affairs separated. Since he wasn't getting what he truly wanted, he completely removed his presence from my children's lives. That hurt me immensely and my son even more because he missed being with his sons. Although we were hurt, I wasn't upset with him for long. I tried to maintain a friendship with him as I thought he was interested in helping with my son's career. Unfortunately, he continuously made it difficult to coexist. So, instead of giving up on my son, I persevered ahead by myself.

CHAPTER EIGHT

When he first started rapping, there were a few family members who didn't understand what I was trying to do. They didn't like that I was always on the club scene. To many people, it appeared as I was partying and clubbing. My sole reason for constantly being in various clubs was to build relationships to further his career. Some of them weren't supportive because they felt my guidance was skewed and I should have encouraged him to be a doctor or focus on his football career. It didn't matter what anyone had to say; his career came first!

Even some of my friends didn't understand my mission. There was a time, one of my best friends invited me to a gathering. It was a conflict with the timing because a professional football player had an event scheduled the same day. I knew important attendees would be there, so I went to network. Ironically, my friend's husband attended the same event. When she found out, she was upset because I chose to network instead of attending her cousin's gathering with her. My decision to support my son caused a rift in our twenty-year friendship. At the time, she didn't understand that his career took precedence over everything. I realized people don't always understand your vision. Because of what I'd been through, I instilled in Yazz that sometimes people can't see the route you're taking to your destiny.

Fortunately, I had the support of my immediate family. My brother was a photographer, and he did our filming. Whenever he couldn't attend, my cousin Isaiah would often film our shows. He also captured the before and after shots as well. My late sister, Sapphire, couldn't always be there, but she called and prayed for us often. Eventually, my mother began attending his shows too. She cheered for him and tried to recite his lyrics when he performed.

While I was grooming him as an artist, I was also teaching him the business as well. I even suggested that he stop calling me 'Mom,' and use a name that made people respect me as his manager. I felt in business women already had struggles, so being viewed as just his mother and not his representation was unacceptable. He agreed and decided to address me as 'Ms. Berry' from that point forward.

Yazz and I always had a close relationship. It wasn't about him being a mama's boy, but about me protecting him. I didn't want his young decisions to affect him years later. We had many disagreements about him getting tattoos. I kept telling him that marking his body limited his opportunities for job offers. I knew I couldn't be with him twenty-four hours a day, but I prayed that he understood my vantage point.

***

Yazz was still having behavioral issues, he wouldn't take his medicine, and refused to do his homework. One day while at his grandmother's house, she pulled out all of her medications to show him that even though he had a disorder, his life wasn't over. She empathized with him as a person with ADHD. She often said, "I have to take my medicine every day just to be okay." I recognized that she was trying to help him. She further explained to him that the condition he has is on his father's side of the family. Then, she named a list of people in the family with the disorder, but she never had her children diagnosed. His father wasn't diagnosed until he was serving a prison sentence and they performed testing.

I wanted Yazz to spend more time with his father's side of the family. When his uncle was released from prison, I felt it was a good idea for them to get to know each other. He called me, at a time when I was experiencing a rough period in my life. Although I was going through something, I needed my son to see that someone else cared about him. His uncle did as much as he could for him. I knew he was trying to get himself together as a parolee, so quality time with Yazz was greatly appreciated. He showed his nephew, unconditional love, but he just wasn't around all the time. If his father cared more about him, he would've been there to help.

Yazz's first mixtape was released when he was fifteen. In the beginning, when he started rapping, his grandmother wasn't fond of it. But she drove him to the studio to help out because I had to work. I think it was hard for her to see him become older; he was always her baby boy. She was so excited, even though later on, she was diagnosed with cancer.

She was ill but remained supportive. Sometimes she couldn't make it to his shows because she was getting chemotherapy. That didn't prevent her from calling to tell him to have a good show, in which she did before he went onstage. When she became very sick, I prayed hard to God that I would be able to spend more time with her. When I took my son to her house, she encouraged him so much. He respected and loved her because of the nurturing and loving relationship she took the time to build with him.

She always told him to play his CD so that they could recite his lyrics together. While she was enjoying her time with him, I was in the bathroom crying because it was hard to see her that way. No matter how tired or ill she was, whenever we walked through the door, she lit up and smiled. It was her way of showing him that the disease wasn't going to keep her down. One thing she always said to Yazz was that he was going to be a star.

There were also times that she would talk to him about his father. He asked her a series of questions that I couldn't answer. He asked, "Was he angry? How does he treat his other kids? Does he love me?" She was very transparent with him. His grandmother explained his father's illness to him and told him that his father's behavior and non-support had nothing to do with him. She even told him not to be like his father. She prayed with him a lot and apologized for his father's absence many times.

I was at work during her last hours. I received a call from Yazz's uncle telling me that he didn't think she would make it through the night. Immediately, I left work and went straight to the studio to pick up Yazz. He asked questions all the way there. He was afraid and didn't know what to expect. I waited until we got closer to her house before I told him that her condition worsened. When we arrived, he pulled a chair up close to her and held her hand. He kept saying, "I'm going to make you proud of me. I know you think I don't listen, but I do. I do. I do." A couple of hours later, she quietly passed away.

At the funeral services, my son sat with his father. He hadn't spoken to him in quite some time. As his father began to cry, Yazz gave him support and comfort. I stood back and allowed him to be the good son that I raised him to be. I always reminded him that he only has one father. My son didn't speak to him after that, but that was a choice that he made. Now, he was much older, so I allowed him to make his own decisions. Besides, his father wasn't trying to contact him, so I didn't want him to feel pressured into building a relationship with him because his mother passed away.

***

There were times I had to mentally shut Yazz out, but it wasn't to the point where he recognized it. I asked the kids to give me an hour or two and then I went to my room. That was the only way I could decompress. I often felt like I was dealing with my pain in motion. But I faced it head on and dealt with it. I always tried to help him understand his disorder, hoping that maybe he would realize how it affected me and everyone around him. I told him that there were going to be people who didn't understand him; therefore, I showed him how to cope in public.

There were even times where I felt like they needed me too much, especially Yazz, but I could never bring myself to say those words to him. I always had to be there for him. I was all he had. Sometimes, I didn't want the responsibility of being a parent. It was so hard, and I felt like I was always in survival mode. But I was losing my energy and strength. I remember the days and nights of wailing and crying. Many times, I went into Yazz's bedroom, got on my knees, placed my hand on his chest and prayed over him. Then, I went to Brianna's room and repeated it. Once I was finished, I went back to my room and prayed again.

***

By the time he was in eleventh grade, I wanted him to explore his options. College isn't for everyone, so my advice to him was if he didn't have plans of attending then he needed to learn a trade. I wasn't going to force college on him. As long as he had plans on being productive, I was going to support him. I also told him that just because he didn't attend college at eighteen didn't mean he couldn't do it later. However, I did speak to him about at least considering a few business courses because he wanted to become an entrepreneur. I told him if his plan weren't paying his bills after a year, then he needed to attend a trade school.

It just so happened that his entertainment career catapulted and he was able to do what he loved. That made me realize that raising your children the way society dictates isn't always the best method. You have to let go and let God take the reins. Psalm 46:10 says, "Be still, and know that I am God; I will be exalted among the nations, I will be exalted in the earth."

Up until that point, I did what was best for him, and it worked out well. All of Yazz's life, I had to create a way for him to conquer everything. There was no cookie cutter formula, and there never will be one. If he decides to attend college someday, I want him to master whatever he studies. Even if he only takes a few classes at night, that's great too because he'll always have something to fall back on. But if he continues on his path and doors continue to open for music and television, then he will still have my full support!

***

I was always concerned that Yazz would get involved in the street life. I checked his phone, his pockets and asked him questions all the time. As teenagers, I gave him and Brianna random urine tests. Before he changed schools, I made him stay in the house until I came home.

Yazz friends were mainly the people who were with Team Yazz because he was always working. That's how the business is. I believe the way I raised Yazz was preparing him for the life he would be living. God was guiding me to make the right choices.

I knew when he started performing that he was going to be a star. There's a documentary with professional tennis players, sisters Venus Williams and Serena Williams, that shows their father being strict. They weren't allowed to do much outside of practicing tennis several times a day. They missed out on similar things as my children - playing outside with friends, hanging out, and having slumber parties; all for the sake of their purpose. Perhaps that's why it was all happening - there was a greater purpose. If God allowed Yazz to experience all of those tribulations, then He had a bigger plan that even I couldn't understand. Today, I realize what it was, and I know that all my hard work and overprotective ways are justified.

***

One Sunday I remember attending church, and the Pastor called individuals to the altar for prayer. I had recently told myself I wanted to put my children on the altar and God led me to church. The night before, I was exhausted and wanted to sleep in late with the kids. That morning my inner spirit urged me to get out of bed. When the Pastor said, "Are there any members here that need prayer?" I ran to the front! He hadn't even finished all he had to say before I was standing right there. I fell to my knees and broke down crying. He prayed over my children and me, and I recall him saying, "Your son will be fine." Hearing that made me feel so relieved. The entire church covered us that day. When the Pastor was finished, he told us just to stay there, but step to the side. I felt like a burden was lifted off of my shoulders. Immediately, I felt stronger, and all I kept saying was, "Thank you, Lord! Thank you, Lord!"

Yazz even said that he felt like we should pray together more as a family. I was amazed at God used him as a vessel to spoke those words. I always prayed with my children, but after that day we prayed together even more. I sensed things starting to change. There would be hard times to follow, but I knew The Lord would be right by my side.

CHAPTER NINE

Throughout the five years he played football, I only missed two games. I remember cheering him on and wishing that I had someone with me to support him as well. When it came to my daughter, I masked a lot of pain. It hurt knowing when she visited her father's house; she saw how he interacted with his family. That made her feel like she was the stepchild. I blamed myself because I believed I should've made better choices in the men I dated.

Behind closed doors, I felt like I was drowning. I had very few people encourage and tell me that I was doing a good job. I wasn't seeking any accolades, but remaining strong was becoming harder and harder. Whenever I thought that things were getting better, life would knock me back down. I remember calling my mother and asking her to keep the kids for the weekend so that I could have some time to myself. I spent the entire day alone, crying and praying. I was thinking of activities for Brianna because Yazz played football and ran track. Unfortunately, I was unable to enroll her in any because after paying the bills; the remaining money was utilized to support her brother.

I wasn't raised in a household with parents who were affectionate, and always verbally expressed their love for me. Of course, my parents let me know they loved me and did an excellent job raising me, but they did it their way. I realized I was repeating those same actions toward my children. I did so because I didn't want them to think that I was weak. I felt inordinate affection and saying 'I love you' often made me appear that way.

Once we were consistently attending church and praying together, I changed my thought process. Every night before they went to bed, they came into my bedroom, gave me a hug and told me they loved me. I quickly noticed a change in Yazz. It was evident that he was receptive to my love and affection and it made him feel better about himself. Children often imitate what they see and hear. When I told him I loved him and reinforced it with my actions, he reciprocated it. I knew it wasn't going to fix everything in an instant. My hopes were, it would shed light on some progress, and it did.

***

Selecting a school that honored his IEP was a battle within itself. I transferred Yazz to West Catholic Preparatory High School, a private co-educational school located in the University City section of West Philadelphia. He secured a football scholarship, and I was only required to pay $200 monthly in tuition fees. The tuition would have been more than double the amount, so I was excited to enroll him there. I knew he would receive a quality education, so my only concern was his ADHD. As soon as he began school, I received several phone calls from most of his teachers, demanding an emergency meeting. During the meeting with the head of the school and the teachers; the principal bluntly told me that if he had ADHD, he didn't belong at their school. They refused to honor his IEP and didn't have to acknowledge it because they were privately funded. Their school wasn't bound by the conditions of the school district. He was only there for three months, and because of his bad behavior, he had received the maximum number of demerits for a student.

In the middle of the week, they informed me that I had to find a new school. I felt discriminated against because of his disorder, but I couldn't dwell on that and needed to make a quick decision. Since that happened during the school year, most of the charter schools were already at capacity. I knew he couldn't attend another Catholic high school because they wouldn't accept his disorder. It was stressful trying to find a school that supported his condition and accommodated the IEP standards. While I searched for a new school, he stayed with my mother until I had the situation rectified about a few weeks later. I didn't want him to attend West Philadelphia High School, so I fought for him to attend a division of Overbrook High School.

While at the school, he had an incident. He was working diligently on a project, but he was unable to finish it at home. He took his supplies to school in hopes of completing it there so that he wouldn't be penalized. He had scissors, glue and the remaining items needed to complete the project. The school had metal detectors, so once he walked through, the alarms sounded. The alert indicated he was carrying something not permitted on school grounds. They took him into a room, searched, and found the scissors. Scissors were considered a weapon, so they took immediate action and proceeded with a suspension. I explained thoroughly why he was in possession of the scissors. I held a meeting with the principal, which was unsuccessful. Subsequently, I had to retain an attorney. Unbeknownst to me, the students were informed about the items they were not permitted to bring into school. This was the one rare occasion when his ADHD worked in his favor. With all that he had to remember, not being allowed to bring scissors into school was quickly forgotten. He didn't remember, and it was an honest mistake. He thought he was doing the right thing by bringing them so that he could finish his uncompleted project.

At the time, they wanted to expel him, but in Pennsylvania, you are awarded a free attorney when your child has a disorder like ADHD. We fought the case and won, but he had to transfer to a different school. At his new school, he had more balance.

He was relocated to a school that assisted students with ADHD in Downingtown, PA, approximately thirty-three miles west of Philadelphia. Although the school fees were expensive, they provided financial assistance to cover the full tuition, because of his disorder.

CHAPTER TEN

As he became older, my biggest problem was with the girls he befriended. Especially, when he started sneaking them into my basement. I resorted to installing a security system and locking the back door with a key to prevent him from coming and going as he pleased. I needed to have a peace of mind. Many times, I set my alarm for three in the morning just to do a room or house check. Brianna would always be in her room, but he would have the pillows under his covers as if he was there. I would call his cell, demand that he came home and warned him of the consequences of his actions. Some occasions he came home immediately, others he didn't. Once it took him forty-five minutes to return. I was beyond frustrated because I had to be up and ready for work in less than two hours, so instead of going back to bed I stayed up and prepared to start my day. The two hours came and went in no time. When I went out to my car, I couldn't believe what I saw. Yazz had driven my car that night, and dented one entire side. It was in no condition to drive, and I had to call out from work. I later found out that Brianna's friend would park the car for him each time he would sneak it out, and that's why I didn't know he had been driving my car.

I was so hurt that I didn't even talk to him right away. I felt like it was a losing battle. Irrespective of what I did to keep him from sneaking out, from installing an alarm to locking doors, he found a way around it. I now know that part of his problem was that I wouldn't let him do a lot of the things that other children did. I sometimes think because of my fear; he felt like he didn't have a childhood. But whenever I would think of easing up a little, something else would happen to make me realize that my fears were not unfounded.

After one of his performances, just as we arrived home, a car that I did not initially recognize pulled up behind us. It wasn't long before I realized that it was those same guys that used to harass us and want to fight him after school. I could immediately sense the tension in the air. Team Yazz was in our car, and the guys who were in the other car started getting out of their respective vehicles. Yazz was ready to fight, but I was against it. I had been around long enough to know how these types of situations ended.

Now outside of their car, the guys from the other car began reaching under their shirts, and my nervousness increased tenfold. I started crying and pleaded with my son to calm down. They knew that he could defend himself very well. He didn't have any problems doing it; so I knew before they even reached for their waistbands that they were armed with guns. For whatever reason, the guys left, and we went inside the house.

It wasn't too long before they returned, walking through the alley wearing hoodies. They stood outside screaming that they were going to shoot my son. As my mind raced to how I was going to get him out of the house, I warned them that I was going to call the police. Then, it occurred to me that my car was parked on the corner of my block. I ran outside, pulled my car up to the house and I instructed everyone to get in the car, before speeding off.

We stayed at my mother's house that night and every other night for the rest of that week. They guys kept an eye out for my son, but they were unaware that due to his heavy involvement in rap that he spent much of his time at the studio. Unbeknownst to them, that's how they would miss him whenever they were looking for him. Situations such as these were precisely why it was imperative for him to listen to me and not sneak around. I wanted him to realize that he couldn't beat a gun and that he could lose his life in an instance. I had hoped that the problems with the guys were over after Yazz had run into them at the store some years prior, and nothing happened. But there it was two years later, and they were back.

It was evident at that point that these guys weren't going to stop until they were able to cause harm to my son. Some time later, my extended family and I were outside my home, waiting to see Brianna off to her senior prom. Once the party bus that she and her friends would be riding in arrived, I noticed that the guys were standing in the alleyway across the street. Sensing my discomfort, one of my cousins walked over and asked them what they wanted. They were bold enough to say they were looking for Yazz. It goes without saying that my cousin did not care for that answer. If I didn't want this to get out of hand, I knew that I had to do something. Needless to say, it would all end badly. I let the guys know that as long as they didn't step on our side of the street, in front of my house, there wouldn't be any problems. I had already filed police reports and tried my best to de-escalate the situation, but they didn't seem to care about any of that. I further let them know that if anything happened to my children or me, the police knew everything about them and their parents; and they would be arrested.

When things seemed to have settled, it was too good to be true. I now had to worry about both my children. Due to my son's rising popularity, a group of girls accused Brianna of thinking that she was better than them because her brother had relationships with local celebrities. That was the furthest thing from the truth, but it didn't stop the girls from thinking it.

One day, I received a call from the school informing me that Brianna had gotten into a big fight. It was revealed that, one of Brianna's girlfriends came to her defense when the group of girls confronted her, and she in turn, helped her friend. The principal wanted to expel them both, but because Brianna had never been in any other trouble, they only suspended her. I don't know how I made it through those times; I can only assume that it was the grace of God that got me through.

CHAPTER ELEVEN

Yazz's behavior became unbearable. I made a decision that I knew would dramatically change all of our lives. He was around sixteen, and at this point, he had been sneaking out the house continuously and fraternized with the wrong crowd. He also wasn't taking his medication at this point. I knew I had to make a tough decision, and it was the hardest thing for me to do. The night before the day I sent him away, I couldn't sleep at all. I was afraid and worried about how he was going to feel. But I knew that if I didn't act quickly, I was going to lose my son to the streets.

Having him admitted to a mental health treatment center was one of the hardest things I had to do in my life. One of my best friends told me about the institution. The facility is located in Delaware, which is about two hours away from where we lived. The center specialized in working with children with severe ADHD, autism, and children who attempted to hurt their parents or themselves. My friend told me that she had taken a position there and if I wanted to bring him in for an evaluation, she would look after him for me.

The next day, I came home from work and Brianna was watching television in the living room. Yazz was in his room with everything in disarray. I told both of them to get their coats and to follow me. He asked me where we were going and I told him that we had an appointment. When we got into the car, I locked the doors because I knew that he would try to jump out and run if he was aware of our destination. As I was driving to Delaware, I tried talking myself out of it. All the reasons why I should take him compelled me to keep driving to get him the help that he needed.

On my way, I prayed the entire time. I asked God to show me what I needed to do to help him. I asked myself, *Did I exhaust every option before coming to this decision?* The answer was 'yes.' I knew he would get reevaluated to make sure that he was on the proper medication and the adequate amount of therapy sessions. As soon as we arrived, Yazz began to ask more questions, but at this point, we were already inside the facility. Once you're inside, you're locked in. The only way out was when they pushed a button and allowed you to leave. I looked around and wondered if I had made a huge mistake.

Even though the staff at the facility was welcoming; the facility wasn't. It felt cold and distant as we were escorted down the hall. I remember turning around to look behind me, and I saw a few children with horrified expressions on their faces. The reality of what I was doing began to trouble me. I felt Brianna gripping my hand as we finally stopped at a desk to start the admission process.

Once he realized what was happening, he said, "Mom I don't want to be here." I explained to him that I was afraid that the things he was doing at home would get him hurt or even killed. When his name was finally called, they evaluated him and decided that they wanted to treat him as an inpatient. That meant that he had to remain in their custody for at least two weeks. I told them everything that was happening, but he kept denying it. I couldn't believe that even at this point, he still wouldn't accept responsibility for his actions.

He told the doctor that he never stole my car and that he was taking his medicine. Once they said that he had to remain there for two weeks, he was crestfallen. Then, he became irate and created a scene. I asked the doctor to give me a minute to speak with him, but Yazz refused to talk to me.

As they walked Brianna and me back to the front, I asked to see the room he would be occupying. They told me that he would see a therapist and a psychologist. He would also be forced to take his medicine. As I walked out the door holding my daughter's hand, I knew that I had made the right decision. I refused to let Yazz ruin his life by getting arrested or killed. My daughter didn't fully understand why he was being admitted. She asked me why he had to stay there alone. I told her that he needed help that I couldn't give him and as a parent, I had to make the decision to protect him. We were both were crying, as I drove away. I knew Brianna was upset with me because she didn't speak to me the entire ride home. Although I knew that I was doing the right thing for my son, I felt empty inside, leaving him there.

I thought to myself: *Is he afraid? Is he going to hate me? Is he going to think that I don't love him?* I was worried about him because he had never been away from me for that length of time. The next day, even though I didn't want to, I had to return to work. I cried while I was driving to work because it hit me so hard.

During the time he was there, me, my mother, and daughter went to visit him. I called to check on him three to four times a day. I couldn't talk to him directly, but I spoke with the nurses.

On one visit, they had him wearing a white jumper, so I brought him some clothes to be more comfortable. He was allowed to wear sweatpants, but I had to remove the strings from the waist. Even his footwear needed the laces removed. We had to walk through a long corridor just to get to him. As we passed the other rooms, I saw children with helmets on. Once I spoke to him, he wanted to know why I put him in there. He had never witnessed other kids trying to hurt themselves. It was shocking to him because he didn't understand the other children's actions. His roommate banged his head on the wall so much that they moved Yazz to a different room.

After being there, he promised he would do better when he returned home, but it wasn't that simple. We had to delve to the root of the issue and then address his behavior. Days lapsed, and he only had three days remaining, which he said felt like weeks. I prayed that he would view the experience positively instead of negatively.

After two weeks of being away, I allowed him to come back home. When he returned, he literally kissed the ground because he was so excited. He said that he was ready to change and he would show me. In the beginning, he showed improvement. He was listening to me, performing better in school and going out of his way to show me that he wasn't the same anymore. That lasted for about eight months, and then he returned to his previous ways. He wouldn't do any of his chores and began sneaking into my room and his sister's room. Soon, I was tired of coming home to an endless battle. I already knew physically disciplining him wouldn't work, so I installed a lock on my bedroom door to have some peace in my home.

Once I placed the lock on my door, he started climbing through the window to get inside my room. His behavior was becoming uncontrollable again. I felt he was trying to teach me a lesson by showing me that I couldn't prevent him from doing whatever he wanted to do. I tried everything I thought of until I was out of options.

Again, while we were in therapy, he denied that he was sneaking into my room. Before I decided to readmit him into the facility, I called one of his football coaches and asked him to come over and speak to Yazz. He chose not to talk to the coach. I didn't want to go through the admission process again, but the situation called for drastic measures. I knew that if I sent him back, he would hate me. As I was contemplating my decision, I decided I rather have him safe and alive. I felt that if he indeed hated me, God would restore our relationship one day.

After crying and praying all night, it was time to take him back to Delaware. This time, I asked the coach to accompany me. The coach almost had to force him to get into the car. Once we arrived, they did an evaluation and decided to keep him for three weeks this time. His coach talked me through it, encouraging me as I executed the papers once again. He explained to me that I was giving Yazz a second chance to get his life together. The coach wanted to visit him while he was there, but my son was so angry, that he didn't want to see anyone. After three weeks, I allowed him to come home. He was home for about four months when I began to notice a decline in his behavior. He was even sneaking girls into my basement again.

I couldn't take it anymore, so I took him back to the institution for the third time. This time, as I was driving, he tried to get out of the car because he was familiar with the routine. When we arrived, he jumped out of the car and took off running! I chased after him in my car, but he was running full speed. I tried to see where he went, but I couldn't find him. I panicked when I realized what had just happened. My son was gone; I was in disbelief.

We didn't have another choice but to call the state trooper to help locate him. It took them forty-five minutes to arrive on the scene. Once there, we looked everywhere, and there was no sign of him. I had never experienced anything like that before. The state troopers had the dogs and helicopters vehemently searching for him. We were near Christiana Mall, a shopping plaza, located between the cities of Newark and Wilmington. We looked inside to no avail and then asked a few employees at a nearby hotel. By nightfall, we still hadn't found him. The state troopers told me that I had to remain there just in case they located him. There was no way I was going to leave Delaware without finding my son.

The hotel, in which I stayed, allowed me to stay one night at no charge because they felt compassion for me and my situation. Later that night, I went back out to search for him because I couldn't sleep. The next morning, the state troopers told me that they still hadn't located him. A few hours later, I received a call from a young lady who lived in Upper Darby, a small township bordering West Philadelphia. She was my son's friend and let me know that he was with her mother at their house. I asked her how he got to Upper Darby, and she said, "He walked to Newark, Delaware and my mother sent a cab to pick him up." Then, I learned that her mother called DHS, the Department of Human Services, which deals with the abuse and neglect of children. Once I arrived at their house and picked him up, I took him directly to Chestnut Hill Hospital in Philadelphia to have him examined. I didn't even have the energy to punish him for scaring me in such a way.

During the examination, the doctor confirmed there were no signs of abuse. He informed the police officers that there weren't any indications that Yazz had been abused, so they put it in the report. When I went to DHS in Upper Darby, they didn't pursue the allegations because they were proven to be false. I could've lost my job because of the accusations, so I had to clear my name. I later received a letter from DHS exonerating me because there was no abuse discovered after their investigation.

After that incident, I tried to take him to a facility in Pennsylvania, but he refused to be admitted. Luckily, I found one that treated him as an outpatient. They were already familiar with him because he went there for therapy. The therapist explained to him that if he didn't follow their instructions, they would call the other facility in Delaware and agree to have him admitted again. I tried to get him to recognize that his behavior and lies affected other people. Although he didn't say that I abused him, he told the facility that he wasn't doing anything wrong. That made it difficult for them to help him.

He had been admitted three times in one year, but after that, I decided not to have him admitted any more. It seemed like the more he was occupied with sports and music, the less time he had to get involved with negative activities. Every season after, he was played sports, and focused on his music.

***

Time passed and Yazz's high school graduation was finally upon us. After successfully completing four years of high school, he was blessed to receive his diploma from the Overbrook school system when he graduated. He was genuinely excited to march in the commencement ceremony, especially since he hadn't been able to participate in his eighth-grade graduation. There were times where he didn't think he would make it to that point and neither did I. But he did, and the pride that radiated from me couldn't go unnoticed. There were people in his family that didn't finish high school and him graduating was a generational curse that he was breaking. He didn't have a criminal record nor had he ever been incarcerated. Seeing him walk down the aisle in his cap and gown was a sight to see. My baby, my son, was a high school graduate.

Philadelphia native, Dr. Marc Lamont Hill gave the commencement address which focused on the period in his life when he was homeless. He told the graduating class how when he dropped out of Morehouse College and became homeless, it was another homeless man that made him look into himself and realize that he needed to be back in school. And he did return. Moreover, he went on to graduate with a doctorate. The moral of his speech was if the graduating class wanted to accomplish their goals, they would have to keep pushing through any adversities they faced. It was as if he was speaking directly to Yazz. After the ceremony, Yazz and Dr. Hill had the opportunity to speak one on one for a brief period. Yazz walked away from their conversation so inspired that he weaved excerpts from Dr. Hill's speech into his next mixtape.

CHAPTER TWELVE

Yazz was coming into his own more and more, and his growth in music proved that to me. I was starting to understand the importance of God's timing when it came to Yazz's life. If it weren't for his past experiences, he wouldn't be the artist and entertainer that he is now.

Initially, when I decided to become Yazz's manager, my protective instinct increased tenfold. As always I wanted to be the best for him, and in the early stages of his career, that's exactly what I was. But I always made it clear to him that if he ever found someone that could manage him better than me, then I would step aside without hesitation. I didn't want to be the reason why he didn't make it or why he only made it so far, hence I maintained professionalism and didn't allow my emotions to get in the way. I only required that they be a positive influence in his life and always put his interests first. I also requested that I remain a part of the team in some capacity.

The day arrived when he became concerned with the level of success I could help him obtain. I wasn't upset and didn't take his concerns personally. I assured him that I would always support his decisions. I understood that it was his brand and that he had to make the best decisions for himself. He knew that I helped him get to that point, but to get him further, I realized I needed more assistance. If Yazz was going to be as big as I thought he would be, I understood that meant I needed to step back and let someone else manage him. However, I wasn't going to abandon him, so I still wanted to have a significant role because I always had his best interest at heart.

Two years before Yazz auditioned for *Empire* the time came when he began to embrace the possibility of new management. After one of his performances, we were approached by a gentleman who was interested in co-managing Yazz. For the next two years, the gentleman and I co-managed his career. At the end of this period, Yazz was almost twenty, an adult, and came to the conclusion that he wanted his mother to be his mom and not his manager. After a few deep conversations I agreed, and together we decided that I would be his business manager while the other gentleman served as his manager.

I viewed the change as a positive not only for Yazz's career but also for him as a man in general. With his new manager, I saw all the possibilities for a positive male influence in his life. I thought that as a man, he could help shape Yazz in ways that as his mother I couldn't. He would be around my son 24/7, and I was holding him entirely responsible for Yazz. I was passing along the torch, entrusting my son in his care. I wanted to make sure that I was making the right decision. I prayed about it and hoped that things would work out. To be honest, in the beginning, even with me accepting that I was no longer his manager, I wasn't entirely happy. There was a part of me that still wanted to oversee his career and ensure that all was running smoothly. It was definitely a hard adjustment. Little did I know that it wasn't the only adjustment that I would have to make in our relationship.

I missed much of my earlier adulthood, having children so young. I had to make every decision with their needs first taken into consideration. I think this played a significant role in my reluctance of letting go of him. The feeling I had, took me back to the early days of me managing his career. Specifically, to when I first realized that the dynamic of our personal and business relationships had shifted. We used to eat together, hang out together and do business together. Now, things had completely changed.

By the time I accepted that he had grown from a boy into a young man, he had already developed into an adult. Since he was older, I had to take a step back. Yazz had to have his experiences independent of me. He had to make his own mistakes and arrive at his own conclusions. He was now charged with making his own choices, and I had to learn how to live with that.

As parents, sometimes we may see things that our children don't, and we try to protect them from anything that may hurt them. It's our job and something all parents have to do at some point, but we have to let go of them when it's time.

CHAPTER THIRTEEN

Throughout Yazz's career, even in it's earlier stages, he was always mindful of the positive influence that he could have through his music. When he was still an unsigned artist, he along with his team, had the idea to start a school tour in Philadelphia. Being as he was unsigned, I was unsure how we would make it happen. That is until we met a gentleman from a program called *Fed Up For You*, who had started a school tour in New Jersey, and was already hosting events for many of the state's schools. After familiarizing ourselves with each other, Yazz was able to join the *Fed Up For You* tour. He loved it, and after seeing the effect the events were having, Yazz informed me that he wanted to do a school tour that focused on anti-bullying. Without delay, I jumped into action, proud that he wanted to help other young people and stand behind a cause with which he had a personal connection.

When I initially contacted the schools, I was met with a lot of rejection. As I heard more and more no's I became discouraged. After a series of rejections, Yazz took the cause upon himself. He arranged a meeting with a principal who had rejected my request, to which he arrived dressed in a suit and tie with his laptop to show them recordings of previous performances. After seeing what he could do and discovering what he was about, the principal scheduled a concert for him at the school. I was awestruck and full of pride. I couldn't believe he was able to get their permission. The best part of it all is that first yes, led to many more from over fifty-one other schools.

Yazz's school tour was at no charge to the schools; we only asked for twenty dollars to cover the expenses of travel. After a while, it got to the point where he was performing in front of six hundred students. As they sat captivated by Yazz, he would speak about bullying, share his views on it and how wrong it was, but he never let them know that he was bullied. His message to them was that they should never, for any reason treat people badly because they look or act differently. I think the message resonated with the students because of Yazz's sincerity and it was coming from someone they could relate to.

I beamed with pride at each of his school performances as I sat back and watched how the students responded to him, particularly since he had gotten into the school himself. At the completion of each of his shows, there would be a line of students waiting to take pictures with him and get his autograph. It was refreshing to see his dreams coming true. He had worked hard to get to that point, and his positive, uplifting content was just what those students needed. From his ingenuity when booking the school tours to his earnest message to the students, I knew that regardless of any naysayers, things were only going to go up from here.

Then came the day we heard Yazz's music on the radio. Power 99 radio host and DJ, Cosmic Kev heard one of Yazz's songs and loved it. He couldn't stop playing it. He decided to put the song into rotation on his show for weeks. One of the first times we heard Yazz's song on the radio, we were sitting at home reviewing material for his next show, while the radio played in the background. In the middle of our discussion, we noticed Yazz's song playing and began dancing. Together we started calling everyone we knew, telling them to turn on the radio. Afterward, we were home every day by eight and listened to Cosmic Kev's Showtime, to see if the song would play again. It did. It played for weeks, and soon other radio stations began to play the song as well. I was so appreciative to Cosmic Kev for the opportunity, and I told him. His response to me was that Yazz had earned it. I knew then that I was definitely raising a star.

As he grew as an artist, his performances reflected his maturity. He handled adversity and technical issues like the pro that he was. There was a performance at the TLA where Yazz's backing track failed while his special guest was on stage. The room unexpectedly went silent as the music cut, and he emerged from where he was waiting backstage. As soon he touched the stage he announced, "We're not going to worry about this," and began freestyling a rhyme. He continued as if the music still played until, in fact, it did. The crowd went crazy! The guest artist picked up on Yazz's vibe, the energy of the crowd, and the two of them continued the show. I think that was a part of who he was becoming as a man. Little things that would have bothered him in the past suddenly didn't seem so important to him. He let much of it just roll off of his back.

Time passed, and my ex-fiancé and Yazz began communicating again. Even though they were in communication with each other, my son still missed having an older male he could speak with sometimes. A few months went by, and my son's hard work positioned him in a place that changed all of our lives. By the grace of God, he landed the role of 'Hakeem' on *Empire*.

When it was time to meet with my son's attorney during his negations for *Empire*, I was unable to accompany him, due to a conflict of interest. But guess who was right there? Lisa! She went in my place to lend her support to him. Other than me, she was the perfect person because he trusted her and was comfortable with her being there. Finding genuine friends isn't easy, and when you're in the entertainment industry, it's even more challenging. Somehow, God managed to connect Lisa and me so that I wouldn't feel like I was going through this life alone.

CHAPTER FOURTEEN

Yazz's most heartfelt and impactful show was performed at the TLA. The studio wasn't large enough for our entire team, but we functioned in it as best we could. People recognized the effort we put into his shows, so pretty soon we started performing at different venues. He began performing at the TLA often and was booked for other shows throughout the city. During one of his performances, he wanted to pay tribute to the late Trayvon Martin by riding a bike onstage wearing a hoodie. I thought it was a great idea, but we had differences about the bike. I felt that the promoter wouldn't let him do it because he had already given me a hard time about Yazz doing a three song sound check. My son was persistent in doing the show the way he envisioned and convinced me to let him do it. I finally listened, and it was one of his biggest shows to date.

One of Yazz's greatest moments came later in 2015 when he was contacted by Philadelphia rapper Meek Mill. He and Meek had history; they knew each other from recording at the same studios. Typically Meek didn't like people he didn't know well in the studio while he was recording, but with Yazz, it was different, and Meek took him under his wing. Years later Meek was still showing Yazz love. He called and invited Yazz to perform at his Welcome Back concert, the most anticipated concert of the year. It was unbelievable. He had never been to a concert, let alone performed at one. I can still remember someone saying to him, "I can't believe the first concert you're going to is the one you'll be performing at." By the time the day of the show arrived, he had rehearsed until his set was pure perfection. His excitement was palpable, and my nerves were wrecked with anticipation.

When Meek brought my son out on stage, he performed the song, "Drip Drop" acapella. This was right when Empire was airing, and the crowd was familiar with the song. While on stage Yazz took the opportunity to freestyle a bit to show everyone that he could rap. At the end of his twenty-minute set, it was impossible for either of us to be any happier. His performance was incredible; he felt it, I felt it, and the crowd felt it. He came off of the stage to supporters just wanting to be near him. They grabbed at him and touched him as he walked by. He was in heaven. He retreated to the dressing room that Meek had arranged for him and took it all in.

The year before only a few people knew his name as an artist, now, thousands were screaming his name. To see him on stage at the Wells Fargo Center was a sight to behold and I rejoiced at the moment. As his time at the

Welcome Back concert came to an end, he told me that he was thankful that I managed him and that I did a great job with his career. This was the first time he'd ever said this to me, and it meant the world to me for him to acknowledge that. It was as if all the hard work that we put in had finally paid off and he felt as if he was finally leaving his footprint on the game.

To commemorate all of Yazz's success, I brought all of the family and many of the people who were an integral part of his career together to celebrate him. The room was filled with individuals who nurtured him, loved him, protected him and saw greatness in him when the rest of the world may not have been able to. We gathered around Yazz in a circle as the Bishop of Yeshua Church prayed over him.

At the conclusion of the prayer, everyone shared their story of how they came to know him and how much he had grown; not only as a person but as a man as well. The room overflowed with emotion. Yazz was humbled by the outpouring of love and thanked everyone for being patient with him. I can't speak for everyone, but it was my pleasure to see him mature the way he had and have the opportunity to meet the gracious and resilient person who stood before me that day. It was a wild ride, and not without its fair share of difficulties, but for him and Brianna, I would do it all again. I had long ago accepted that God's way is always best, even through trying times I know He never makes any mistakes.

Yazz concluded his acknowledgment and appreciation of everyone, turned to us all and said, "People think that when you become a star that you change, but it's the people around you that change. Don't ever treat me like I'm not Bryshere Gray because I'm not going to act like that." In those two brief sentences, he reminded me that everything that I had instilled reflected in the way he talked and carried himself. His transition to adulthood may not have been flawless, and yet he was the perfect version of himself. I knew right then that I no longer had to worry about him as I had in the past.

Our time as mother and son had been an assignment from God. It wasn't about being perfect or having all of the answers. It was all about both of us being able to depend on God and strengthen our faith by leaning entirely on Him. To this day, Yazz takes pictures with his hands clasped in a prayer position, and his head bowed. He knows where his help comes from and I'm proud that he never forgot. Yazz's purpose is bigger than a show, a song or fame. His purpose is about showing other children with a disorder, any disorder, that they too can be everything that God created them to be. As a mother of a child with a condition, my purpose is to encourage other parents that when they reach the end of their rope; to remind them that there isn't anything that God places in front of them that they can't conquer. They must trust that storms don't last and eventually run out of rain. Just believe until you make it out on the other side; grow through what you go through.

Family and prayer have been two constants in my life, and I've always tried my best to instill the importance of family and God in my children. Through it all, they have been my saving grace, and I firmly believe that they are what brought Yazz through to be the great man that he is today.

CHAPTER FIFTEEN

As his mother, I always saw something in Yazz that set him apart from others. I saw on a daily basis how kind, thoughtful, hard-working and talented he was. He couldn't always see it because he wasn't trying to be special, it was just who he was naturally. However, just as I saw the spark in Yazz, others saw it as well.

I recall the time that he left the Batcave and began recording out of another studio. The gentleman with which Yazz was working saw the star quality he possessed and proposed a deal where he would receive fifty percent of everything that he earned in the future. It goes without saying that neither Yazz or I saw this deal as a good fit, and the contract remained unsigned. But the situation served to show the importance of understanding that he was more than just a talent. He was a business, and many would look at him as such. All things considered, this was expected, but it was imperative that he took the time to familiarize himself with the inner business workings of the entertainment industry. I made sure as I went along, that he learned the business with me. I didn't want to run the risk of him being blindsided if ever there was a time I was not with him. I wanted to put him in a position to have ultimate control of his career. He may not have known it at the time, but I was setting him up to have longevity in a business that often chews people up and spits them out without a second thought.

Thankfully, as a result of my days as a manager to Kimo and others, I was prepared for many of the obstacles and issues that arose during my time as his manager; not all parents are experienced. They often ask me for advice on the best ways to support their child's interest in the entertainment industry and how to handle it once they become a star. What I tell them is as follows:

First and foremost, be sure that your child is well-rounded and prepared for whatever opportunity that comes their way. Fully develop your child's skills and avoid putting them in a box. That's not to say that your child has to be able to do everything. However, if they can sing, enroll them in voice lessons. If they can also dance, enroll them in dance classes and so on and so forth. The entertainment industry is fluid, and often one sector of the industry melds into the others. Therefore, your child's blessing may not come from one particular talent or another. This is what happened to Yazz. His first love was rapping, and his big break came acting on a television show portraying a rapper. Had he not honed his acting skills, he may not have had the great fortune of portraying the character of Hakeem on *Empire*.

The entertainment industry is often a world of make-believe, where people are fooled into believing their own hype and the lies of others. Inspire them to be confident and never arrogant, and to stand in the morals you've instilled in them. Never be afraid to say or hear no. It's just a word; it doesn't define your child or their talent.

Encourage your child to network like crazy. Despite their age, it's never too early for your child to develop mature, respectful and grounded relationships.

You must accept that there will be sacrifices to be made; some bigger than others. Don't let that deter you. If the end goal is important to you, the sacrifice will be well worth it. Teach your child that they too will have to make sacrifices and at no time should they become too attached to anything in the ever-changing entertainment industry. There will definitely be times when you have to make a tough decision and pass on an opportunity. There will be other times when it's your child that will be the one passed over. Don't take it personally. In fact, don't take anything personally. You and your child will be affected by things without so much as an explanation as to why or what happened, but you will survive if you remember that it's not about you, it's merely the nature of the industry.

By all means, make sure you read every line of every contract. If you're able to, hire an attorney to avoid getting lost in the small, critical details of a contract. Don't let your child sign their life away or let anyone position themselves to take everything your child worked hard to gain.

Above all, you have to allow your child to be a child. In the new millennium, children grow up so fast. And if your child is in entertainment it's worse because although they are children, they hold the job and the responsibilities of an adult. Make sure that in addition to being professional they enjoy themselves. A part of enjoying themselves includes being comfortable in who they are and how they look. One of the things that Lee Daniels, the co-creator, executive producer, and director of *Empire* said to me, was that Yazz had a very clean-cut look. I knew to deter him from excessive markings on his body. Do what you can to protect their image.

Many times, it's a dream come true for them. Always remember that in spite of it all, whether your child is new to the industry or has been involved in it for awhile, achieving dreams are supposed to be fun. Never let the pursuit of a dream become a burden. Most importantly make sure that the desire to be in entertainment is their dream and not yours.

My ultimate advice to any parent whose child shows an interest in the entertainment industry is to stay vigilant. The world is a crazy place on its own, but with the added aspects of money, power, and fame, it can be ruthless. As parents, we are our children's first line of protection, regardless of their age. This applies doubly to parents of children in the entertainment industry. We are too, no matter the scenario, have their back and ensure that the people around them have their best interest in mind, at all times. It is our responsibility to vet those who we chose to let work with our child. The world is full of real life monsters, some of which who want your child's money while others want their innocence. You have to do all you can not to let it happen.

Not all parents will decide to manage their children, and that's understandable. This is exactly why I established, Ms. Berry Cares, my foundation. Ms. Berry Cares was created to encourage, empower and educate parents. Over the years I have acquired a strong skill set geared toward artist development, and it is what helped get my son to where he is in his career. I have chosen to focus primarily on managing children because I love working with them and as the name of my foundation suggests, I do genuinely care.

Furthermore, experience has taught me that there are unscrupulous people who prey on parents desperate for their children to become stars. I set out to offer parents a better option with Ms. Berry Cares. I will hold workshops that will inspire parents to be a part of their children's careers because it's all too important that they are present. I invite parents to come on board so they can feel comfortable knowing that they have someone in their corner who cares. I want Ms. Berry Cares to represent morality, honesty, and professionalism. I made some mistakes along my way, and I've learned from them. Some things I would have done differently in this industry and I want to share with parents my knowledge so that they may better assist their child on their way to stardom. Having been on both sides of the coin as a mother and a manager, I am well-equipped to prepare parents for whatever may come their way.

Whether or not you, as a parent, decide to manage your child's career, make sure that they put forth their best effort, and as a parent, you do the same. The entertainment industry is like any other thing in life; you get back exactly what you put into it. Every decision will not be perfect, and you can't control every outcome. Never feel guilty if you've given your best. Teach your child to do the same. Make every decision wisely. Educate yourself and your child. Be sensible, yet never be afraid to take risks. Don't ever give up. Remember those that helped you and your child along the way. And most importantly, put and keep God first.

The often forgotten side of being the parent of a celebrity is the change in attitudes and treatment by those around you. Current societal conducts had programmed many people to believe that our worth as people is connected to who we know or how much we have, and if what we have is the latest and greatest. Therefore, it is a natural progression for those who subscribe to this way of thinking to assume that if you are fortunate enough to have come in contact with fame or wealth in any way that you will look down on them. Anyone who has ever known me knows that this is the furthest thing from the truth. Not to mention, that my son's fame is his fame, and my self-worth or how I view others is independent of it. Nevertheless, there is always at least one person who uses the clichéd reasoning to take issue with me.

I've been at my job for sixteen years, and I've worked on the same floor for fifteen of those years. Suffice it to say when *Empire* began airing; the staff was well aware that Yazz was my son. Everyone, regardless of their race, watched and still watches the show. An attending physician often came to me and discussed the latest episodes. He even occasionally brought in news clips about the show that I hadn't seen.

Along with the increased popularity of *Empire* came a shift in the dynamics between my coworkers and me. People began hanging around my desk more often, and they suddenly became more friendly. Colleagues who I never had much of a relationship with asked me to hang out with them, but I respectfully declined because I wanted all my friendship connections to be genuine. It became incredibly hurtful. People who I had cordial relationships with suddenly attempted to insert themselves into my inner circle; not based on their opinion of me, but because of the notoriety of my son.

For others, it caused them to have a certain disdain for me. There was an incident where I forgot to transfer a patient. The mistake was innocent and a byproduct of my focus on another one of my duties. For my oversight, I was called into the office by my manager. Of course, it was only after my error was pointed out to them by a co-worker.

I immediately had an idea who it was and eventually asked the individual the reason she spoke to the manager before speaking to me. I was aghast to find out that she thought I had intentionally not transferred the patient. We weren't long into our conversation when she mentioned the show and shared that she thought I was always talking about my son at work. I couldn't believe what I was hearing. From the way she spoke to me, it was as if she waited for the opportune moment to throw Yazz's success in my face; like I should be ashamed.

Don't get me wrong, I am very proud of my son, but it was others who initiated conversations about the show. Of course, I engaged in the conversation, as it would be rude not to, but I never initiated it, nor did I come to work bragging about him. I tried to explain this to her, and that I had no way of controlling what others wanted to discuss. Her response was to blatantly ask me why I was still working if my son had it so good. As one would expect, I immediately ended the conversation.

The truth is, the entire time they were filming the pilot I never told a soul at my job. It wasn't until a year later, when the episode premiered, that people realized my son was in the series. They asked me why I didn't say anything. I figured that when it was meant for people to know, they would.

To this day, I still come in contact with people who don't understand why I'm working if my son is famous. It's as if they can't comprehend that my support of Yazz's career was never about him taking care of me. It was about him achieving his dreams.

I've always wanted both of my children to be in the position to take care of themselves. That's what parents are supposed to do. I'm a healthy adult; I can take care of myself. I've always been independent, and I love my job. Instead of taking care of me, I told my son to invest his money. My promise to myself was to push them to follow their dreams and to be all they could be in life, which is one promise that I was able to keep.

ANDRIA MAYBERRY

AFTERWORD

The Real Life *Empire*

In preparation for this book, I had to call upon memories that had been buried deep in the recesses of my mind for years. As they came to light, the resemblance between Cookie, the onscreen mother of Yazz's character Hakeem and myself, were not lost on me. At times the similarities are uncanny; the absenteeism, the business savvy and the undying love for my children.

With everything I've experienced in my life, if there is one thing I would have done differently, it's not having missed so much of my children's youth while working. Logically speaking, I know that it was something that I had to do, but emotionally it's tough accepting that my absence played a role in how my son would come to view me. For the most part, there was a lot of resentment toward me for me having to work so much. Looking back, I can now see how much I wasn't there, and it hurts. Whether it was to get my children everything they wanted, to make sure that the bills were paid and we had food to eat; I was always working. If life was perfect, things could have been different, I could have been home more, but the reality of the situation is that I couldn't. I was a single mother, and I had to do what needed to be done to provide for my family. The strange part is I didn't realize how much I wasn't physically present with my children until I started writing this book. When I was

185

at the moment, I knew that I worked long hours and I knew that my multiple jobs often kept me away from home, but I couldn't see it. It wasn't clear to me then. My time away is what helped us to sustain life; it was a necessity. I looked at it as work, not spending time away from my children. Even now with my seeing it all more clearly, I don't have any regrets about working to provide for my family, but admittedly I would've done things differently. I've accepted that a lot of Yazz's frustration with me was because of my absence and how I handled things when he was growing up. He was simply crying out for my attention and some quality time together.

LETTERS
TO MY
SON

Dear Little Yazz,

I'm writing you this letter, praying that God will open your heart and clear your mind to allow understanding to take place. When I became pregnant with you, I was young. I had no idea what being a single parent of two children would entail. I can tell you that, although I was scared, and didn't know how I was going to take care of you and your sister, I was happy to have you. It was then that I knew I had to grow up. I know that I have made some mistakes along the way. But I believe that I tried to do the best that I could do for you and your sister with the limited resources and education that I had. I have always put you and your sister first. My goal as a parent was to make sure my children had food to eat, a roof over your heads, and that you were safe.

Although you may have felt as though I was punishing you with some of the things that I put in place to keep you safe, I didn't know what else to do. I felt as though I was going to lose you to the streets. I didn't want to visit you in prison or bury my son. So, at times, I became desperate because I was so afraid that I was losing you. I was very uncomfortable watching you behave in a manner that I couldn't prevent from happening sometimes. If I could have the results would have been very different. I pray that God will help you to understand during your transition from a little boy, to a teenage boy, and to a young man. I hope that you see that I accomplished what I set out to do and that I was saving your life. I wanted to help you become a productive citizen in society and keep you from being a statistic. I will always continue to lift you up in prayer and ask God to cover you. Yazz, know that I do love you to the moon and back!

—Mom

My King,

As I am writing you this letter, I'm thinking about you from birth all the way to twenty-three years of age. I remember the first time you walked, and the first time you said, "Mom." I remember your first day of school, your first move up day, your first touchdown, the first time you ran track, the first time you scored a point in a basketball game, the first time you got hurt in a football game and had to get surgery, the first time you lost a close friend, the first time you went to your prom and when you graduated from high school.

Then, I remember the first time you touched the stage, the first time I heard your song on the radio, the first epic performance, the first award show, the first audition for a TV role and the first call you got from Lee Daniels when you were told that you got the role as Hakeem, on *Empire*. For all of those moments, I've been right by your side. I've watched you grow from a little boy to an intelligent young man. I've witnessed you overcome some of the things that society said you were not supposed to accomplish. I've always instilled prayer throughout your journey and the importance of not letting anyone put you in a box. I know that sometimes things were rough, but as promised, I knew you would be okay.

I am very proud of you. I pray that God continues to soften your heart; to give you the discernment to know when there is negative energy present, and the ability to get rid of it. To give you wisdom, strength, courage, understanding, peace, stronger faith, and a stronger family unity. For your family will always be there when no one else will. All of these things will continue to mold you into the great man that God is building you to be. Stay humble, appreciative and keep God first and your family second. I love you!

—Mom

If you or someone you know is a victim of domestic violence, please contact the
National Domestic Violence Hotline at **1-800-799-7233** or visit their website at **www.thehotline.org**

If you or someone you know suffers from ADHD, please contact CHADD at **1-800-233-4050** or visit their website at **www.chadd.org**

Andria Mayberry better known as Ms. Berry is a powerhouse in the entertainment industry. Recognized for her tenacity and business savvy as a mother and manager to her son, *Empire* superstar, Bryshere Gray who plays Hakeem Lyon on the hit series. She is currently trailblazing her way as a motivational speaker, philanthropist, emerging sleepwear designer, and now author. For the past 17 years, she has maintained a position in the medical field. She presently oversees three critical care units in a hospital while managing her business ventures. She has recently started her foundation, *Ms. Berry Cares*, which provides resources and empowerment to parents of children striving for stardom. "My calling is to empower and encourage the parents to stay involved in the dreams of their children," Mayberry continues, "I was a single mother holding down two jobs while managing my son's career. I can now take my knowledge and experiences and pass it on to parents that are where I once was." Ms. Berry is the true example of what a mother's love, and sacrifice can accomplish. She will continue her quest to inspire all women, mothers, and fathers to keep pushing, striving, and fighting for their children.

Keep up with Ms. Berry on Facebook at Andria Mayberry and Instagram @msberrybiz.